# Information Architecture for Designers

**Structuring websites
for business success**

**Peter Van Dijck**

"We are at an amazing moment of a Gutenberg-level event, with electronic wings able to fly through understandable information of our own choosing. With Velcro claws, we collect all the data that warm and answer our inherent curiosity and questions. I dream of asking a question, a simple childlike question, and receiving an answer. What a dream!"

**Richard Saul Wurman,
*Information Anxiety 2***

A RotoVision Book
Published and distributed
by RotoVision SA
Route Suisse 9
CH-1295 Mies, Switzerland

RotoVision SA
Sales and Production Office
Sheridan House
112/116A Western Road
Hove, East Sussex
BN3 1DD, UK

Tel: +44 (0)1273 72 72 68
Fax: +44 (0)1273 72 72 69
Email: sales@rotovision.com
Web: www.rotovision.com

10 9 8 7 6 5 4 3 2 1

ISBN 2-88046-731-4

Book design by Eirik Bøe, www.krim.co.uk
Illustrations by Sam Ayres

Production and separation by Provision Pte. Ltd., Singapore
Tel: +65 6334 7720
Fax: +65 6334 7721

# Information Architecture for Designers

**Structuring websites
for business success**

**Peter Van Dijck**

RotoVision

4

 Introduction

 Website strategy

 Audience research

# Table of contents

## Information architecture

## Designing functionality

## Interface design

# http://iabook.com

The website that goes with this book can be found at http://iabook.com ⧉ . It contains useful templates for deliverables mentioned in this book, useful links and additional information, and a sample chapter.

The website itself was, of course, developed using a mix of the techniques presented in this book. It doesn't matter if your website is big or small, like this one. Thinking about strategy, target audience, information architecture, and usability is useful for websites of any size.

The strategy phase consisted of me and the publisher discussing the business value of a website to go with the book. In short, we decided that CDs are out, websites are in. We talked about when the website should be launched, and how we could add value to it in order to drive traffic. We decided that useful templates would be attractive for our target audience (which we had defined before writing of the book had started).

During the research phase, I analyzed other book websites. A quick and dirty method, but an effective one. It turned out there are well established conventions on how these sites are organized: they tend to contain an overview of the book (a table of contents, a sample chapter), errata and updates, reviews, and often additional useful information like links or even extra content. I printed out screengrabs and hung them on the wall, read them and thought about which elements I needed on my website.

Designing the information architecture was easy—small websites like this don't need sitemaps or flow diagrams, just some thinking and good writing. I reserved most of the development time for the writing—writing on the web is different from writing for a printed book, and is too often neglected.

Before going live, we did a usability test to make sure there weren't any glaring problems that we had missed. I invited a few friends who happened to be in the target audience over for dinner, and observed them while they used the website. I made a few small changes after that experience. I hope you enjoy the result.

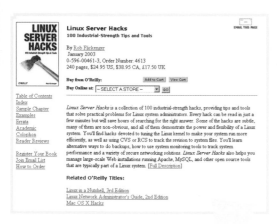

**RESEARCHING SIMILAR WEBSITES**
The research phase consisted of a competitive analysis: I looked at a list of similar websites and analyzed their content and structure. Such research fits in any budget.

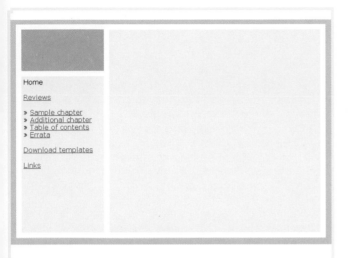

**AN EARLY WIREFRAME FOR THE WEBSITE**
**Really small sites built by really small teams**
**can do without much of the documentation**
**that large sites need. Always weight the**
**usefulness of creating documentation**
**against the time it takes.**

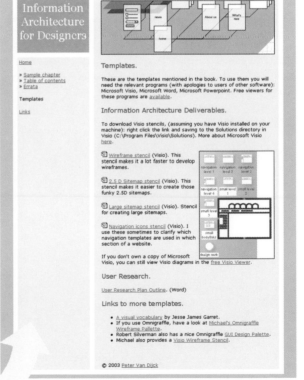

**SAMPLE SCREENGRABS**
**http://iabook.com**

# Author's note

This is a book about information architecture for the web: the art and science of organizing websites so they are easy to use and achieve their goals. The term "information architect" was coined by Richard Saul Wurman in 1975, but people have only recently started calling themselves information architects. Information architecture for the web is a new field: it's been around for only a few years, and the demand for information architects is growing all the time. The field has grown from the need to manage the large amounts of information available on the new medium of the web, and has its roots in library sciences and human-computer interaction.

If you are designing websites and looking for new techniques to make them easier to use and more targeted toward their business goals, this book is for you.

Just like your favorite illustration or HTML-editing program, the practical techniques we discuss are design tools that will make your life easier, your websites more focused, and your clients happier. Even though this book is focused on developing medium- to large-size business websites, the principles apply just the same when creating a personal or an art site. We will call the owner of a website "client" throughout the book, but a client can be someone within the same company, or even yourself, if you are building your own website.

The book is organized around the typical steps that an information architect takes when building a website: plan, research, develop. In the introduction, we'll give an overview of the tools and techniques that information architects use: audience research, sitemaps, task flows, and wireframes. In the following chapters, we examine these techniques in depth: discussing strategy (Chapter 1), doing audience research (Chapter 2), designing the information architecture (Chapter 3), designing the flow of the website (Chapter 4), and designing the user interface (Chapter 5). The chapters are interspersed with case studies describing how information architecture solved design problems in practice.

Throughout the book, you'll find real-life tips for the typical challenges that information architects face: from dealing with the team and the client, and creating efficient deliverables, to incorporating information architecture in your design process.

# Index of tips

# Key

Book web icon          Tip          Attributed quote

# Introduction

# What is information architecture?

Information architecture is a new field in web design. It is different from visual design or programming in that it focuses on the structure of the website, not its functionality or look. This chapter gives an overview of the main information architecture concepts and deliverables—the definable work that the information architect produces. Later chapters expand on these ideas.

The goal of information architecture is to build websites that are easy to use, fulfilling both the client's brief and the aims of the user.

*Information architecture is not about maps and diagrams; it is about communication*

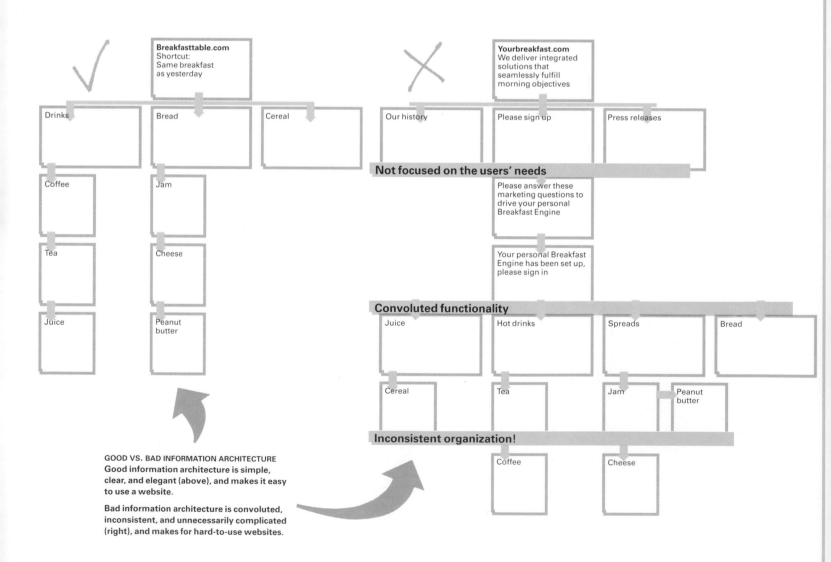

**Breakfasttable.com**
Shortcut:
Same breakfast
as yesterday

Drinks

Bread

Cereal

Coffee

Jam

Tea

Cheese

Juice

Peanut butter

**Yourbreakfast.com**
We deliver integrated solutions that seamlessly fulfill morning objectives

Our history

Please sign up

Press releases

**Not focused on the users' needs**

Please answer these marketing questions to drive your personal Breakfast Engine

Your personal Breakfast Engine has been set up, please sign in

**Convoluted functionality**

Juice

Hot drinks

Spreads

Bread

Cereal

Tea

Jam

Peanut butter

**Inconsistent organization!**

Coffee

Cheese

GOOD VS. BAD INFORMATION ARCHITECTURE
**Good information architecture is simple, clear, and elegant (above), and makes it easy to use a website.**

**Bad information architecture is convoluted, inconsistent, and unnecessarily complicated (right), and makes for hard-to-use websites.**

# What does an information architect do?

The core job of an information architect is to organize the information on a website so that users can find things and achieve their goals. Users will be happier, buy more items, or spend more time on the website, and this makes businesses more money.

Typically, an information architect is involved in:

- User research: what do people want to achieve on the website?

- Defining content and functionality: how will it help the user and business goals?

- Developing organization schemes: how will the website be organized?

- Developing the interface, together with the visual designer.

- Follow-up throughout the building of the website.

The most typical deliverable of the information architect is the sitemap: a structured overview of the website. When creating this structure, the information architect selects from endless organization options, trying to satisfy both business and user goals.

However, creating a sitemap should not be considered the most important thing that an information architect does. Information architecture is not about maps and diagrams, but about organizing information and communication within a team. Because of their intimate knowledge of the users and business goals, the information architect works closely with a number of people: the programmers to determine functionality; the visual designers on interface design; and the writers on the copy. Communication skills are crucial.

Most of the deliverables that an information architect creates are meant to communicate information about the website to the team and the client. The maps and diagrams are communication tools, not ends in themselves. Because the information architect takes such a central place in a web design team, the number one skill of an information architect is listening.

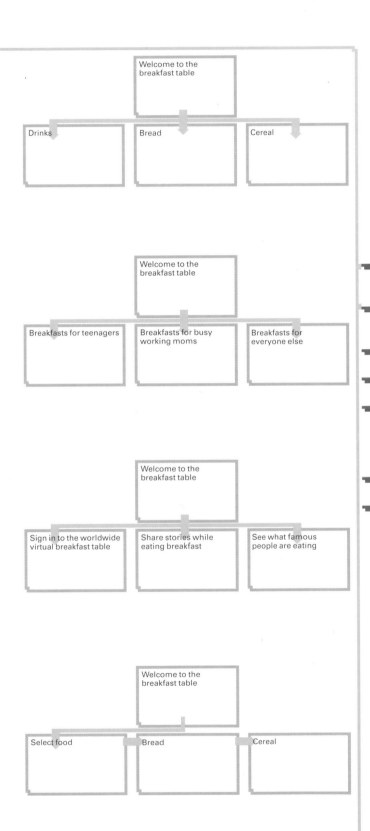

**VARIOUS ORGANIZATION OPTIONS**
There are endless ways of organizing the same information, here are four possibilities.

Business goals and user goals drive which organization schemes are used.
See Chapter 3, page 77, for more detail.

## The user experience

The user experience is the sum of the feelings and thoughts somebody experiences when visiting a website. The visit should be a positive one, involving feelings of achievement and contentment. A bad user experience will drive users away—remember when feelings of frustration and anger have prevented you from returning to a particular website? The information architect is concerned with the user experience. In team discussions, they will often take the side of the user—the person who will visit the website.

When visiting a website, whether we are happy with the visit depends on a number of elements. These include visual design (the look and feel); content (text and imagery); functionality (what it does); and performance (speed). However, none of these will make the visit a positive experience if we cannot find what we are looking for, or do what we are trying to do on the website. The number one complaint about websites is, "I can't find what I'm looking for." The perception people have of a website is largely based on whether they can achieve their own personal goals. This makes good information architecture crucial for a successful website.

To be able to accommodate users' tasks and goals in their design, the first job of the information architect is to really understand who the users of the website are, and what they are trying to do. All design decisions begin with this understanding of the audience. Chapter 2, page 43, explains a number of audience research techniques—interviews, observation, and usability testing—and some research deliverables—audience analysis, personas, and scenarios.

An understanding of user goals has to be balanced by an understanding of business goals. Often, the business will want something different than the user. For example, a business may want to gather personal information but the user may want to protect his or her privacy. The information architect's challenge is to address both these needs. Chapter 1, page 24, discusses strategy and business goals.

## Flow and tasks

The information architect designs websites, not just web pages.

The experience of visiting a website is not defined by one page—it's defined by all the pages visited. Each individual page of a website can be beautiful, easy to use, and rich in content, but if the pages do not work together in a coherent way, the whole experience of visiting the website will suffer. The idea of experiencing a group of pages together is called "flow."

Flow connects pages to support tasks. A task is a planned action on a website, like sending an email, buying a book, or researching a topic. Most tasks require the information architect to design a flow whereby the user is taken through a number of screens to complete the task. Task flows are designed; Chapter 4 explains how. That's why we have to think about the things users will want to do on the website—so we can design flows for them. Tasks can be complex, and contain sub-tasks. The task of sending an email, for example, has the sub-tasks of conducting a spell check.

If websites were designed for one user only, to do one task, it would be easy to design the perfect website. But websites are usually designed for large audiences consisting of many different users, and so must support multiple tasks and sub-tasks. Designing flows to support the most important tasks on a website is hard.

*The information architect designs websites, not just web pages*

*The perception people have of a website is largely based on whether they can achieve their particular goals*

# Deliverables

There is a large and ever-growing list of methodologies and deliverables at the information architect's disposal. This book describes the most popular deliverables: a description of the site in question's content and organization—often in the form of a sitemap—and a functionality description that explains how the website is supposed to work. The level of detail in these descriptions can vary quite a bit. The following section gives an overview of these deliverables, and Chapters 3 and 4, from page 77, will discuss them in depth

**SITEMAPS AND CONTENT TABLES**
The sitemap and the content table are two different ways of showing the pages on a website. They both have their strengths and weaknesses: the sitemap (right) clearly shows structure, while the content table (below) works better for really long lists of content with lots of additional detail. Chapter 3, page 77, provides more detail on both approaches.

## List of content and organization

The information architect is usually responsible for a list of all the content and its structure on the website: this is often presented as a sitemap or a content table.

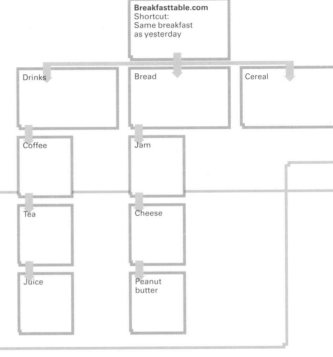

## Content table

| | A | B | C | D | E | F |
|---|---|---|---|---|---|---|
| 1 | ID | Name | Content | Functionality | HTML Template | Notes |
| 2 | 1 | Homepage | Welcome text | Same breakfast as yesterday | A | Functionality to be developed |
| 3 | 1.1 | Overview of drinks | Overview of drinks | Drink selector | B | |
| 4 | 1.1.1 | Coffee | Coffees | | C1 | |
| 5 | 1.1.2 | Tea | Teas | | C1 | |
| 6 | 1.1.3 | Juice | Juices | | C1 | |
| 7 | 1.2 | Bread | Overview of breads | | B | |
| 8 | 1.2.1 | Jam | Jams | | C2 | |
| 9 | 1.2.2 | Cheese | Cheeses | Cheese selector | C2 | |
| 10 | 1.2.3 | Peanut butter | Peanut butter | | C2 | |
| 11 | 1.3 | Cereal | Overview of cereals | Advertising | | |

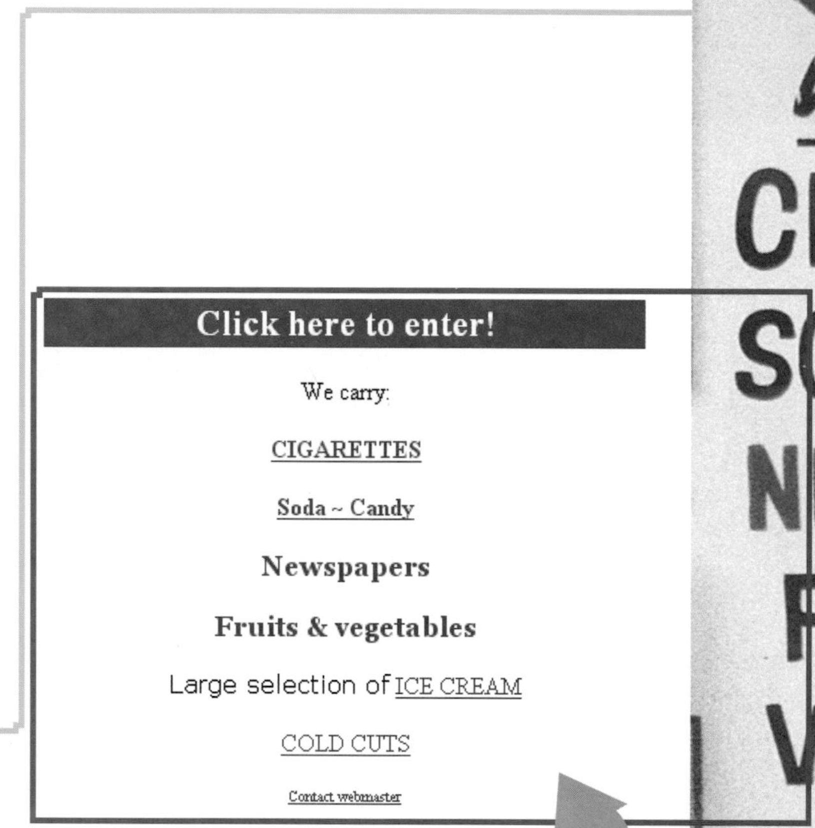

Click here to enter!
We carry:
CIGARETTES
Soda ~ Candy
Newspapers
Fruits & vegetables
Large selection of ICE CREAM
COLD CUTS
Contact webmaster

ENTRANCE
WE CARRY:
CIGARETTES
SODA · CANDY
NEWSPAPERS
FRUITS &
VEGETABLES
large Selection
of ICE CREAM
COLD CUTS
HOURS:
MON-FRI 7-11

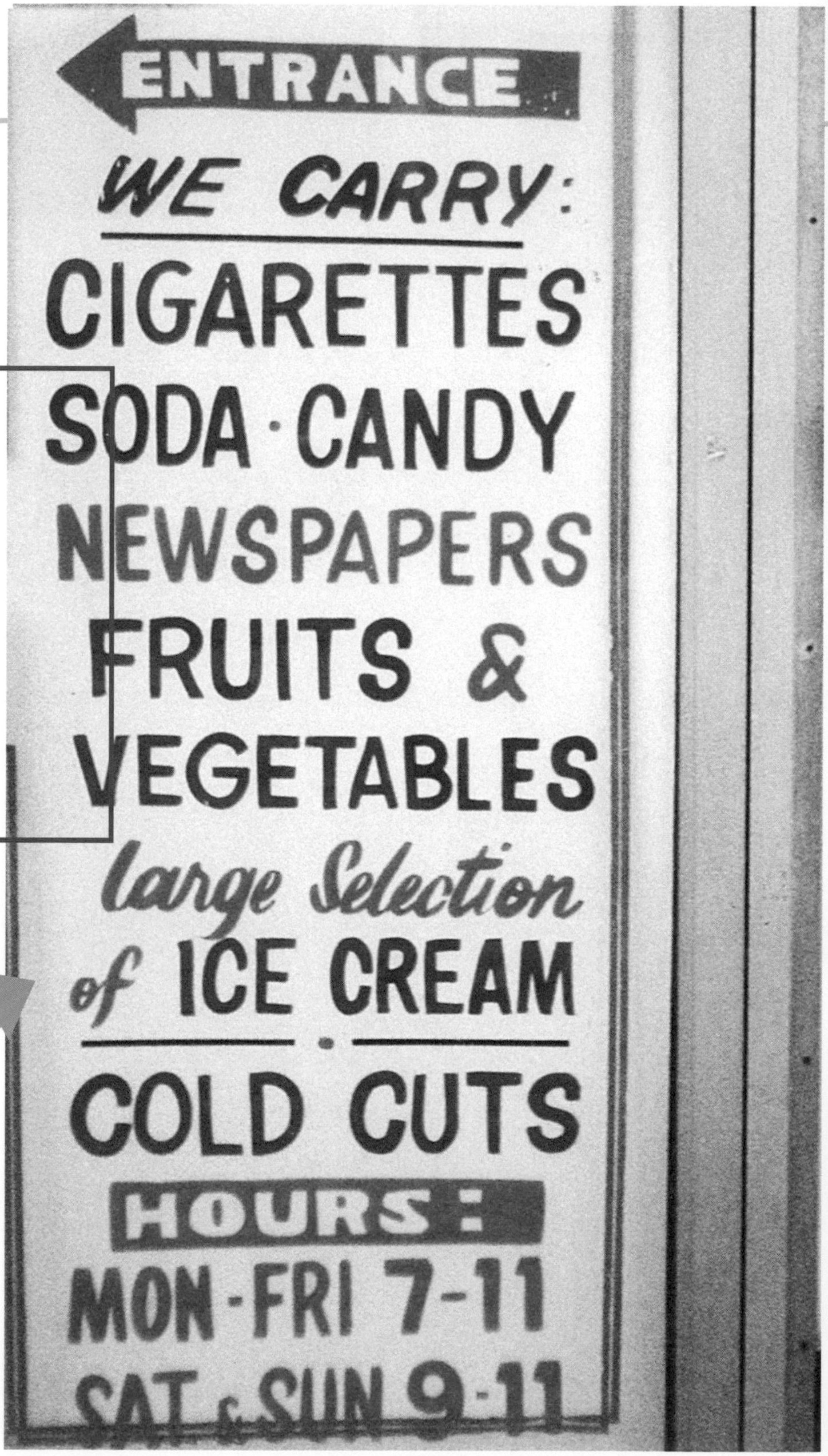

REAL-LIFE INFORMATION ARCHITECTURE

**Early websites often looked as if they were designed for a real-life shop window instead of for the web. Walking down a busy street is like surfing the web. Imagine shop displays to be like homepages and look around for examples of real-life information architecture and design.**

**Websites need a lot more organization than shop window displays however, because it's a lot harder to navigate the web than it is to navigate your high street. The only interaction you have is clicking, and all you can see is a tiny screen of 800 x 600 pixels. It would be like walking around with your eyesight limited to a tiny square, and every time you wanted to move your head you would have to wait four seconds for the scene to download.**

## Description of functionality

The functionality description and task flows describe how the website works, how individual pages work together, and what tasks people can perform. Again, the presentation of this can take many forms, including scenarios and flow charts.

## Wireframes

Like sketches of the user interface, wireframes show interface design without showing visual design. They indicate the buttons, links, content, and other interface elements on a page, and show relationships between the elements on the page. They are developed jointly by the information architect and the visual designer. Wireframes are useful because they let you focus on the structure of the user interface and iterate the design of that, without designing a time-consuming visual design every time.

### Returning user

Persona: Joe

Function: Suggest remembering breakfast

Scenario: Joe likes to have the same breakfast every day. So every day he goes to the website and types in the same choices. After a while, the website notices this, and offers to remember his favorite breakfast. Joe hadn't noticed the small icon that offers that functionality and accepts the offer. From now on he only has to click one link to get the same breakfast.

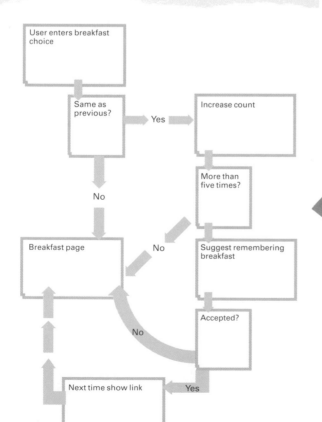

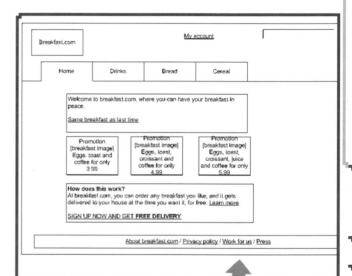

**A WIREFRAME**
This wireframe shows what elements are to go on the page, not the visual design treatment.

**DESCRIBING FUNCTIONALITY**
Different ways of describing functionality offer different levels of detail. Chapter 2, page 44, explains how to use scenarios, as shown top left, and Chapter 4, page 123, explains how to use flow charts, as shown left.

## Conclusion

Information architecture is a set of skills and techniques. Look at each technique as a design tool. The more techniques you have at your disposal, the more flexibility you have when making design decisions. Using these techniques will not mean that design decisions are suddenly made for you. It just means you will have more information to base your decisions on, and additional ways of evaluating a website. Start using these techniques in your web design practice and you may find you have a richer, more complete, insight into what makes a website work.

**IA AS A PROFESSION**
**Information architecture is a young profession, but luckily a very open one. There is a lot of sharing of best practices and exchanging of ideas going on. Here are some of the more popular websites that publish a wealth of interesting articles.**

**WWW.** BOXESANDARROWS.COM
**Boxes and Arrows publishes articles by a variety of writers.**

**WWW.** LOUISROSENFELD.COM
**Louis Rosenfeld, one of the writers of *Information Architecture for the World Wide Web*, has an interesting website with regular updates and thoughts.**

**WWW.** ADAPTIVEPATH.COM
**Adaptivepath, a leading information architecture firm, share their methodology and publish articles on their website.**

# Learning more...

Information architecture for the web is a very new field, but also a very open one: a lot of the top people and companies freely share methodologies, tips, and even templates of their documents.

A few good books have been written, the main one being *Information Architecture for the World Wide Web* by Peter Morville and Louis Rosenfeld. It is the classic book that defined the field.

Other good books include:

*Information Architecture: Blueprints for the Web* by Christina Wodtke

*Practical Information Architecture* by Eric L. Reiss

*The Elements of User Experience: User-Centered Design for the Web* by Jesse James Garret

*Look at each technique as a design tool*

**There are also some excellent websites available:**

**www. adaptivepath.com**
Adaptivepath, a leading information architecture firm, share articles about their methodology and even provide templates on their website.

**www. iawiki.net**
The IAwiki, a community website run by Eric Scheid, holds a lot of regularly updated content about information architecture—this is the place to go to if you are doing research.

**http://iaslash.org**
IASlash was started by Michael Angeles and contains information architecture links that are updated daily.

**www. boxesandarrows.com**
Boxes and Arrows is an online magazine that publishes articles about information architecture by a variety of writers.

**http://semanticstudios.com/publications/semantics/**
Peter Morville writes regular articles about IA.

**Once you start digging around a bit in the information architecture world, you will quickly uncover the existence of fascinating weblogs written by leading information architects such as:**

**http://peterme.com**
(Peter Merholz)

**http://eleganthack.com/blog**
(Christina Wodtke)

**www. noisebetweenstations.com/personal/weblogs**
(Victor Lombardi)

**http://louisrosenfeld.com/home/**
(Louis Rosenfeld)

**www. blackbeltjones.com/work**
(Matt Jones)

20

# Website strategy

## What do business goals have to do with design?

## Discussing business goals

## User goals and tasks

## Measuring success

## Content and functionality

## Conclusion

## Learning more...

Strategy is the collection of ideas behind a website: the high-level plan for realizing the client's business goals. It consists of answers to questions like: what is the business problem we are trying to solve? Why will people visit the website? How will it make money? How will it grow over time? You cannot design an effective website without knowing the answers to these questions, and it is strategy that will shape your design.

Strangely, strategy is often glossed over at the beginning of a project—more attention is given to the more tangible aspects of web development like visual design and technology. When your client starts getting excited about visual elements (the colors on the homepage, Flash animation) or some cool new technology (XML .NET) before you have discussed strategy, refocus the conversation. Talking strategy at the outset of a project is crucial.

Strategy consists of a combination of user goals and business goals, and how you plan to address those. User goals are the reasons people will visit the website, and the things they want out of it. Business goals are the reasons the business is creating the website, and the things they want out of it. Defining these two groups of goals and how they interact is the first challenge of the information architect, and is what this chapter is about.

## What do business goals have to do with design?

Business goals directly and indirectly influence the design of a website. You may feel, for example, that the amount of text on a page is a design decision based on considerations of visual balance and ease of use. Yet during the late 1990s, many websites started splitting their stories into more and more pages, in order to sell more banner impressions, so that a business goal was driving a design decision. What is more, the business goal was in conflict with a user goal—reloading a page eight times just to read one article can get really annoying. When the advertising market changed during 2001 and 2002, this practice was reduced.

Business goals and market conditions have a direct influence on design decisions. To create good design, you need to be familiar with them.

---

### Some questions to ask the client at the start of a project

• Why are you building this website?
  -What are the short- and long-term business goals?
  -Can some of these goals be expressed in numbers?
  (number of visitors, widgets sold, subscriptions…)

• What will the business invest in the website?
  -How much money?
  -Who will work on it?
  (remind them that websites need ongoing attention)

• Why will people visit the website: what are the user goals?
  -Is there existing research on the target audience?
  -Who is the website meant for?
  -Why will the audience visit the website?
  -How will they find it?
  -What will they do on it?

---

**"Strategy? But we want to get to work!"**

When you insist on talking strategy, team members will often resist, saying they "just want to get on with things." Don't give up—having discussed strategy beforehand will save time later when discussing features and design details.

## Discussing business goals

Business goals tend to be about money, but even a non-profit site has business goals. Amnesty International wants its website to increase awareness and get contributors: these are business goals. Your personal homepage allows you to practice your design skills, or showcase your résumé. These are business goals. Business goals are the reasons why the website is being built.

But back to making money, the core driver of most commercial websites. Selling things is an obvious business goal, but also consider the following examples:

• Keeping existing customers happy—it's often cheaper than trying to win new customers.

• Reaching new markets—selling worldwide.

• Decreasing support spending—call centres are surprisingly expensive. Provide customer support on the website that decreases support calls and the site will pay for itself.

• Creating a cost-efficient sales channel—fewer offices have to be built if you have an effective website: online banking is a good example.

• Increasing efficiency in the supply chain—this consists of the companies that supply you with the things you use to do business: automating this can save costs.

• Knowledge management—if department A tries to solve a problem that department B already solved six months ago, a company loses money; an intranet can help avoid such situations.

• Testing new products and brands—testing new products on the web is an efficient and cheap way of testing if consumers like them.

• Lock in early adopters—if you get people to use your website, they will be reluctant to go to a competitor's website as long as they are happy. This is especially crucial for sites that aim to become personalized to the user over time, like personal finance or email.

There are many possible business goals: the important thing is to have the client explain them to you in detail before you start discussing the design of the website. Write them down in a few paragraphs—or have your client provide them—and ask the client to confirm the document.

USEFUL TOOLS
Sticky notes are useful tools: they can be used to discuss business goals with the client's different stakeholders. Organize a discussion session, write down business goals on sticky notes, and sort them into groups. Hang them on the wall so they can be referenced easily.

## Design decisions are driven by strategy

## Even a non-profit site has business goals

"A client was convinced that their website was missing key content, and hired me to do a content gap analysis comparing their lines of business with their information available online. After working with their business units, I realized that they had tons of great content — but nobody could find it. Content findability was causing more problems than content availability. The client realized significant cost savings by some simple information architecture improvements instead of diving in and developing more content to languish buried and unfound."
**Jess McMullin, Information Architect**

**Speak the client's language: learn some business terms**

Learn to use business terms like "Customer Lifetime Value" (the total amount of money someone spends with a company) or "Customer Acquisition Cost" (the amount of money it costs to get a new customer to make their first purchase). Business people have their own language, and to communicate effectively with them you need to speak it. The website ⊡ has links to books and websites to learn more about business language.

**Business goals and the economic climate**

Business goals change depending on the economic climate. When the economy is doing well, businesses are open to trying out new things to expand. Risky projects with a potential high pay-off are popular. When there is a downturn, businesses tend to focus on getting more out of existing investments, so redesigns and optimization projects become more important.

# User goals and tasks

People come to your website for a reason. They want something, and if you do not give it to them they will leave frustrated, vowing never to return. Users have goals; things they want to achieve—like staying in touch with their friends, or saving time in their busy lives. To achieve those goals, they want to complete tasks, like sending emails, or buying clothes online. Answer the following questions together with your client to determine user goals and tasks:

• Who is your target audience?

• What are their goals?

• What tasks will they fulfill on your website?

Note that further research is usually needed; putting these questions to your client is just a first step. You will also need to ask the users—the next chapter discusses user research.

When a business comes to you to develop their website, they usually have a good idea of their business goals. User goals and tasks are often neglected. Discuss them with the client, and write a high-level description—like the following example.

**Key goals and tasks of our target audience**

Client:
Fictional personal investment website

Our target audience:
High-income, working in the USA, between 30 and 50.

Key user goals:
Our audience wants to manage their money more easily than through using an offline bank. They feel they will have more possibilities with an online bank. They want to play a semi-active role in the investment of their money: they do not want to trade stocks themselves, but they do want to keep an eye on how their investments are doing. They want to feel secure, and not spend too much time thinking about it, yet to feel they have invested wisely and will get a good return. They might typically review their investments once or twice a month.

Key user tasks:
1. Learn about the online site and compare it with other online and offline investment possibilities.
2. Make the decision to transfer some or all of their funds.
3. Decide which investment options to select.
4. Transfer their investments to the online site.
5. Track their investments.

Note how the task descriptions don't mention how people will be able to track their investments, just that the website will provide the possibility. This leaves implementation details sufficiently flexible and open while being specific about what needs to be accomplished.

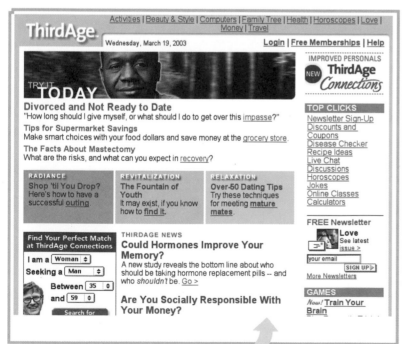

**USER GOALS**
**The target audiences of these two sites are very different, and they have very different needs that they expect the site to fulfill.**

## Measuring success

How will you know the website is successful? You should try to incorporate a few measures for success at the outset of the project. Some typical measures of success are:

● Number of unique visitors: individual people that visit your website.

● Conversion rates: when a visitor does what we want them to— to buy something or subscribe, for example—we have converted them. The percentage of visitors that converts is our conversion rate. If we increase our conversion rate from 5% to 7%, then every marketing dollar we spend to get people onto the website will yield 2% more results.

● Total sales/subscriptions: it seems an easy measurement, but how do you calculate the number of people that would have bought in a shop instead of online?

● Decrease in customer support calls: a new website can decrease support calls and save costs, but be aware that the initial increase in support calls when people are still getting used to the site can skew the numbers.

Defining success or failure in numbers can really help to focus a project. However, if this is the launch of a new website (as opposed to a redesign of an existing website), estimating numbers may be hard. It is easier to use numbers when adjusting an existing website: at least you have the original numbers to make a comparison with.

Measures of success that are qualitative (that do not use numbers) can be useful as well:

● Audience satisfaction: if you are building an intranet, it is easy to poll the audience before and after the new website is up. For public websites, you can poll people in a pop-up or on the homepage. Alternatively, you could contact a small number of people who you know use the website and ask if you can interview them after the launch. See Chapter 2 for interview techniques.

● Third-party reviews: have your website reviewed by an independent third party. Many companies offer usability testing services. Also keep an eye on reviews by consumers on sites like epinions.com.

● When you have agreed with the client on measures of success, write them down in a short document. Ask them to sign this off if you feel they are not taking the process seriously—there is nothing like a sign-off to focus the mind. You can keep referring to this document throughout the project when discussing the website

*Defining success or failure in numbers can really help to focus a project*

**Do you really care about the number of visitors?**

Beware of making the number of visitors the main measure of success on your website. Most websites do not just want visitors, they want converted visitors, and so should use conversion rates as a measure of success. Sometimes exactly who visits your website is more important than the numbers of visits you receive.

If a large oil company creates a website to show their commitment to the environment, they want to reach the people who influence public opinion: activist groups and the press. Exactly who visits that website and the effect it has on them becomes a crucial issue. In this case, tracking their websites, publications, and mailing lists would be an efficient way to see how your website is performing.

**Be careful when interpreting server logs**

Server logs keep track of the number of people who have visited your website, where they came from, which country they are in, and so on. However, if you use this information, make sure you study the limits of server logs first. The internet environment poses severe limits on the reliability of the information that servers gather. Be aware of this or you may be basing your decisions on false data.

**www.** DIMECOMOESTOY.COM

Dimecomoestoy, a Spanish version of Hotornot.com—where viewers rate the attractiveness of submitted portraits and learn the cumulative average rating for that person—has a very simple business goal: to sell advertising. Producing content is free: it consists of images that users upload themselves. The website's only costs are bandwidth and administration. Every page viewed is an ad served, so the website tries to be as addictive as possible: it's really hard to visit this site and look at fewer than three or four pages (just try it). Their business goal is also apparent from the sign-up page (right): they ask for demographic information (age and location) that is used to sell advertising.

# Content and functionality

The content and functionality of a website are: how you address user goals and tasks; how you address business goals; and how you try to reach your success criteria. At this early stage, you should discuss content and functionality on a high level, and avoid getting bogged down in implementation details. Relate each piece of content and functionality to your user and business goals. It is easy to come up with possible features; relating them to goals will help you to decide which ones are worth implementing. Also consider implementation cost when deciding on functionality. A template like the following can be handy. This is also available for use from the book's website ⊟.

### Content table

| A<br>Proposed features | B<br>Business goals | C<br>User goals | D<br>Implementation:<br>cost/time/<br>maintenance |
|---|---|---|---|
| **Mailing list** | 1. Sell advertising | 1. Get information easily without having to visit site daily | Functionality:<br>One-time cost,<br>estimate $8000 |
|  | 2. Get users to visit site more often | 2. Easily unsubscribe or manage subscriptions | Writing content:<br>4 hours per month |
|  |  |  | Managing feedback:<br>4 hours per week |

**When in love with the wrong functionality**

A difficult time in an information architect's life comes when a client is enamored with a certain idea for content or functionality that you believe won't serve them at all. People sometimes cling to their ideas as if they were babies. You can deal with this by following these steps:

1. Refocus the client on user and business goals—make sure they agree to these goals.

2. Do a brainstorming exercise to open their minds to other possibilities. Generate lots of ideas, so they feel their initial baby is now only one of many in the kindergarten of potential features.

3. Have the discussion about which of many possible features to implement. Keep reminding them of user and business goals.

4. Mention money—calculate the expected return on investment of this feature.

5. Use the magic words "phase two". If they still cling to their baby, explain it can be easily moved to phase two, even if you have never talked about a phase two before and nobody has a clue what that might mean. Position the website as something that will be worked on even after this part of the project is finished.

Finally, remember that you as an information architect can easily fall into the same trap. When this happens, work yourself through the steps above.

THE DISCUSSION OF STRATEGY: ONE MORNING, A REAL ESTATE BROKER COMES IN WITH AN IDEA FOR THEIR WEBSITE…

We were thinking of having this "Find a house" feature in Flash. Here's how we think that might look. You could zoom in on a house and then see the price for it!

That's very interesting. Before we discuss the feature in more depth, could you describe the user and business goal that it addresses? That will help me understand it.

THE INFORMATION ARCHITECT CLEVERLY REFOCUSES THE CONVERSATION ON BUSINESS AND USER GOALS…

Well, our users often complain about finding a house. They can't get a good overview of what's available on the market… Also we think a cool tool like this will make us stand out more…

So your users want an easier overview of the available houses, and the business wants to stand out from the competition?

That's right!

Can you tell me a bit more about other problems your users face?

Another thing they often ask for is plans of the house and pictures.

OK…

What kind of information is the most convincing to them? What kind of things do you show them when they come to your store in order to convince them to go on a house visit?

Mostly pictures, and we have these official statistics of the neighborhood as well… and if there's a cinema or something we'll drive them past that, that works well.

So here's a list of elements that seem to convince your clients to call you, or "user goals" as we call them: an easy overview of available houses, plans, pictures, statistics of the neighborhood, and additional info. The way we usually work is to start with these user goals and then come up with ideas of how to address them on the website. Your Flash movie is a great start. It really addresses the goal of getting an easy overview of an available house, although it may be costly in implementation. Next I'd like to discuss how we could address the additional user goals we've identified.

OK, that sounds good.

AND SO THE DISCUSSION WENT ON, THIS TIME FOCUSED ON STRATEGY. USER AND BUSINESS GOALS DROVE THE DESIGN DECISIONS.

After discussing high-level content and functionality with the client, write it down and make sure the client agrees with the description. Keep the functionality description high-level, and focus it on the user: what can they do on the website? Explain which user and business goals the solution addresses. Do not focus the description on implementation details like interface design or technology. Also describe which elements of the solution you believe will require more research or testing. Setting expectations is important.

Shown right is an example of a very high-level functionality description using a personal finance website example. It really only describes the general shape of the solution, and the reasoning behind it. During further research and design phases, this piece of functionality will take further shape. Notice how the example does not discuss implementation details like interface design or visual design. It focuses on user goals and business goals. Also note how it identifies areas that will need testing.

**High-level loan functionality requirements**

The loan calculator will allow users to find out what type of loan they want to take out. It will show different types of loans, and how they work out over time. The user can enter the amount they would like to be loaned; find out how much they would pay every month over time; and how much they will pay in total. The calculator will also give practical, real-world advice in text or audio form with each type of loan, in order to make sure that decisions are not based solely on numbers.

Reasoning:
We believe that other online calculators do not really help people much since our experience in the offices shows us that people do not decide on numbers alone; they decide on their specific circumstances: what other loans do they have? How much money do they have available? What other loans might they want in the future? The text descriptions (which might include focused questions) convey knowledge about these "soft" issues when deciding on a loan type.

User testing will be done, focusing on the additional advice (which format is best—audio? video? text? or combinations of these? How much and what type of advice is needed?) as well as general ease-of-use and conversion rates. We propose two rounds of testing: one doing interviews with sales, to find out the information people ask for; and one testing paper prototypes with users, to find out which type of presentation works best.

The business goals served by this calculator:
To increase conversion rates. In order to measure this, user identities will be tracked and logged throughout their visit to the website, and a special report will be automatically generated that compares conversion rates of visitors who use the tool versus visitors who don't.

*Setting expectations is important*

*Keep the functionality description high-level*

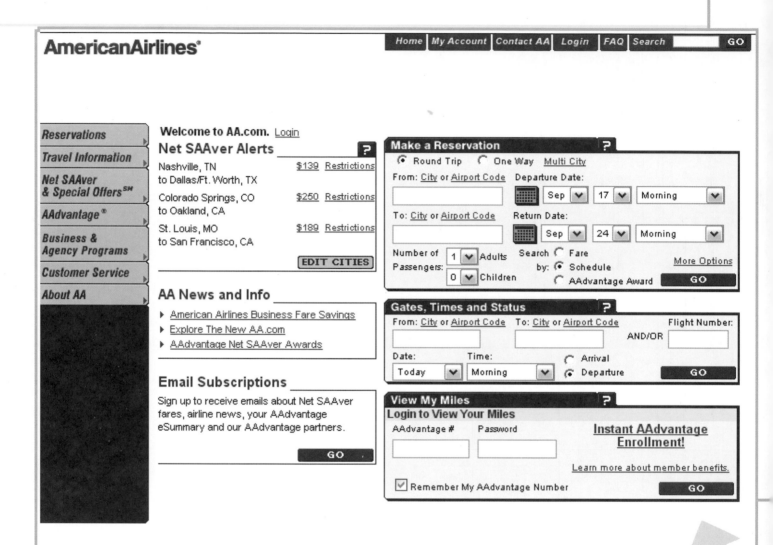

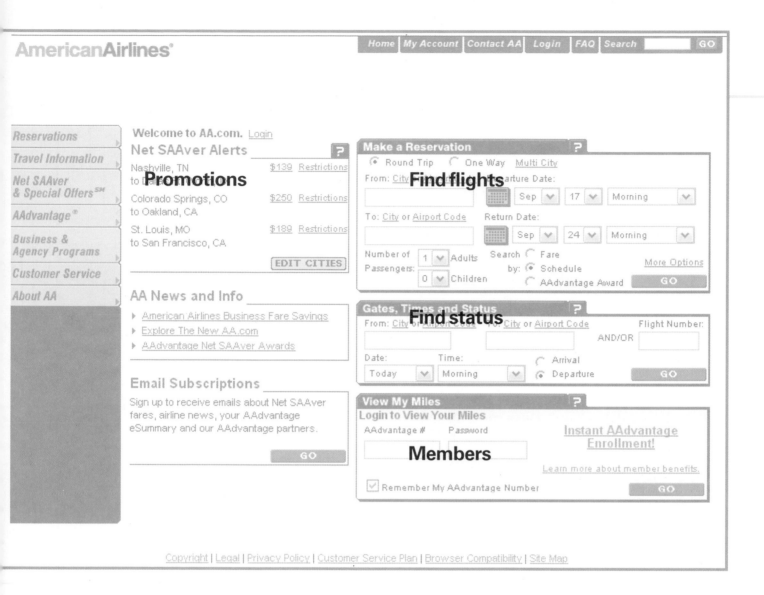

AmericanAirlines®

Home | My Account | Contact AA | Login | FAQ | Search [        ] GO

Reservations
Travel Information
Net SAAver & Special Offers℠
AAdvantage®
Business & Agency Programs
Customer Service
About AA

Welcome to AA.com. Login

## Net SAAver Alerts                     [?]

**Promotions**

Nashville, TN                $139  Restrictions
to D...

Colorado Springs, CO         $250  Restrictions
to Oakland, CA

St. Louis, MO                $189  Restrictions
to San Francisco, CA

[ EDIT CITIES ]

## AA News and Info

▸ American Airlines Business Fare Savings
▸ Explore The New AA.com
▸ AAdvantage Net SAAver Awards

## Email Subscriptions

Sign up to receive emails about Net SAAver
fares, airline news, your AAdvantage
eSummary and our AAdvantage partners.

[ GO ]

### Make a Reservation                   [?]

**Find flights**

⦿ Round Trip    ○ One Way    Multi City
From: City or Airport Code    Departure Date:
[              ]   [📅]  Sep ⌄  17 ⌄  Morning ⌄
To: City or Airport Code    Return Date:
[              ]   [📅]  Sep ⌄  24 ⌄  Morning ⌄

Number of    1 ⌄ Adults    Search  ○ Fare
Passengers:              by: ⦿ Schedule     More Options
             0 ⌄ Children      ○ AAdvantage Award  [ GO ]

### Gates, Times and Status              [?]

**Find status**

From: City or Airport Code    To: City or Airport Code    Flight Number:
[              ]   [              ]   AND/OR   [              ]
Date:          Time:              ○ Arrival
Today ⌄    Morning ⌄    ⦿ Departure    [ GO ]

### View My Miles                        [?]
Login to View Your Miles

AAdvantage #        Password        **Instant AAdvantage Enrollment!**
[              ]   [              ]

**Members**                            Learn more about member benefits.

☑ Remember My AAdvantage Number    [ GO ]

Copyright | Legal | Privacy Policy | Customer Service Plan | Browser Compatibility | Site Map

Comparing homepages of similar websites
can be a good exercise in recognizing how
business goals can influence design. The
three airlines whose websites are shown
on this and the following pages have almost
identical functions on their respective
homepages (find flights, flight status,
promotions, members, and news), and are
all targeted towards consumers. Yet they
have subtly different designs, influenced by
their different business goals.

Note that exercises like these are just
interpretations of business goals—it's hard
to guess why certain decisions were made.
However, it is clear that most airline websites
are converging towards a single, generic
design standard. In the end, only different
user and business goals (including different
brands) will motivate different designs.

 AA.COM
American Airlines' homepage is more
focused on consumers: promotions come
first, while the members section (probably
aimed at business people) is at the bottom
of the page.

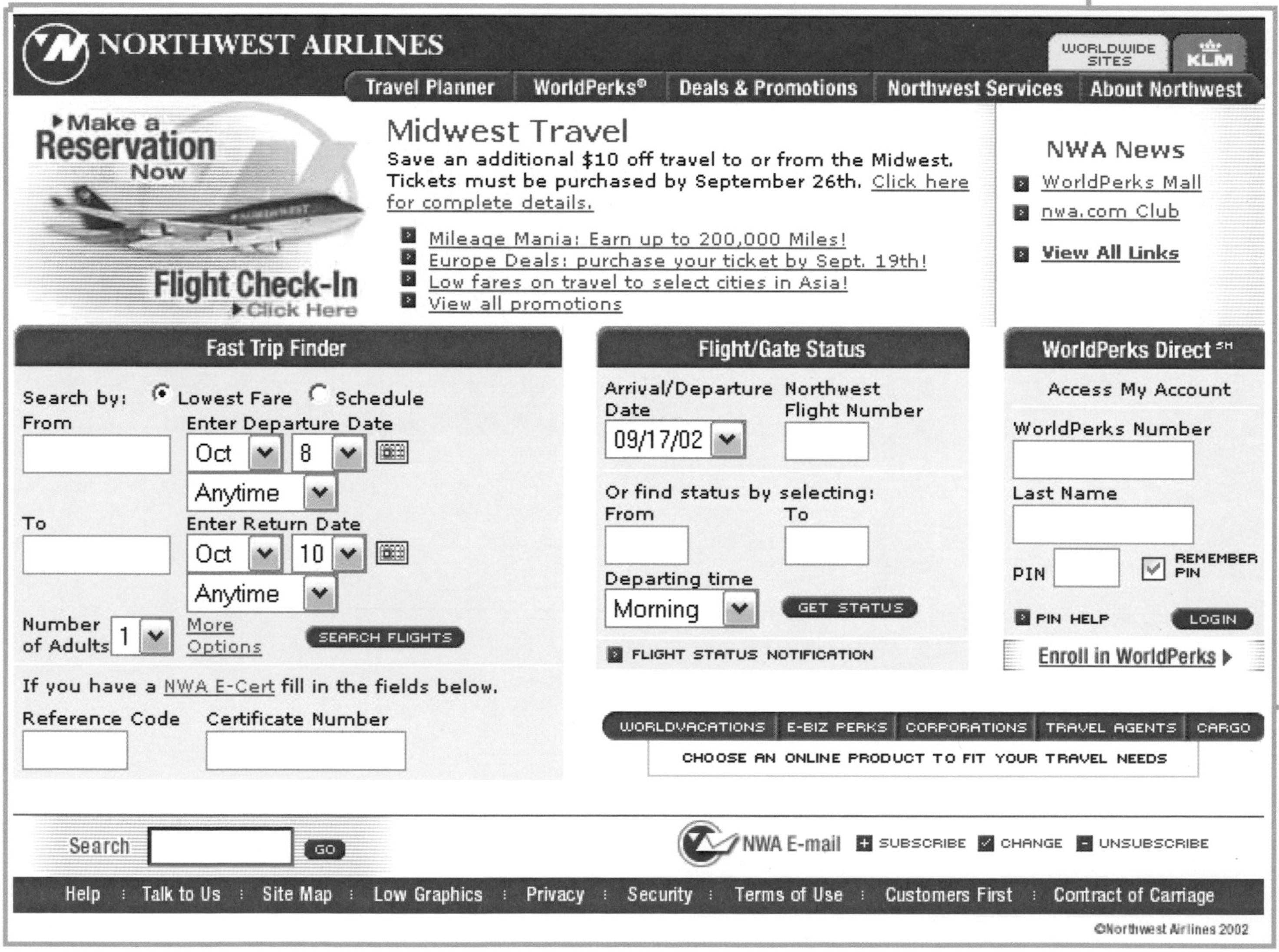

**NORTHWEST AIRLINES**

WORLDWIDE SITES | KLM

| Travel Planner | WorldPerks® | Deals & Promotions | Northwest Services | About Northwest |

▶ Make a **Reservation** Now

**Flight Check-In**
▶ Click Here

## Midwest Travel

Save an additional $10 off travel to or from the Midwest. Tickets must be purchased by September 26th. Click here for complete details.

- ▪ Mileage Mania: Earn up to 200,000 Miles!
- ▪ Europe Deals: purchase your ticket by Sept. 19th!
- ▪ Low fares on travel to select cities in Asia!
- ▪ View all promotions

### NWA News

- ▪ WorldPerks Mall
- ▪ nwa.com Club
- ▪ **View All Links**

---

### Fast Trip Finder

Search by:  ◉ Lowest Fare   ○ Schedule

From

Enter Departure Date
Oct ▼  8 ▼
Anytime ▼

To

Enter Return Date
Oct ▼  10 ▼
Anytime ▼

Number of Adults  1 ▼   More Options   SEARCH FLIGHTS

If you have a NWA E-Cert fill in the fields below.

Reference Code   Certificate Number

### Flight/Gate Status

Arrival/Departure Date    Northwest Flight Number
09/17/02 ▼

Or find status by selecting:
From        To

Departing time
Morning ▼    GET STATUS

▪ FLIGHT STATUS NOTIFICATION

### WorldPerks Direct ℠

Access My Account

WorldPerks Number

Last Name

PIN          ☑ REMEMBER PIN

▪ PIN HELP    LOGIN

**Enroll in WorldPerks** ▶

WORLDVACATIONS | E-BIZ PERKS | CORPORATIONS | TRAVEL AGENTS | CARGO

CHOOSE AN ONLINE PRODUCT TO FIT YOUR TRAVEL NEEDS

---

Search [          ] GO

NWA E-mail  ➕ SUBSCRIBE  ☑ CHANGE  ➖ UNSUBSCRIBE

Help : Talk to Us : Site Map : Low Graphics : Privacy : Security : Terms of Use : Customers First : Contract of Carriage

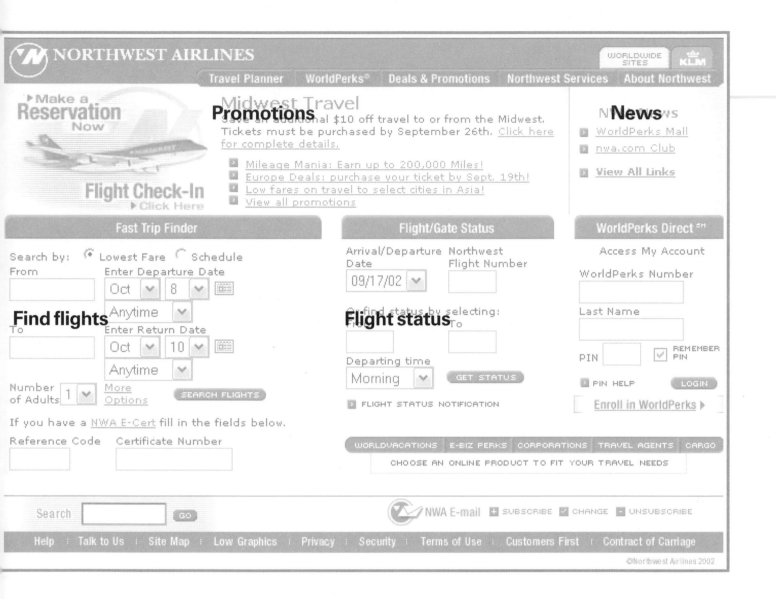

**Promotions**

**News**

**Find flights**

**Flight status**

www. NWA.COM
Northwest Airlines uses carefully worded
labels such as Fast Trip Finder rather than the
typical Make a Reservation and has a Flight
Check In tab, both of which emphasize the
web's focus on speed of use.

*In the end, only different audience and business
goals will motivate different designs*

## Conclusion

The initial strategy work focuses on getting a high-level overview of the project. You define high-level user goals, business goals, and content and functionality. It's important to discuss the strategy for the website in depth before talking about information architecture, visual design, or technologies. Business goals are defined by the client, while user goals and tasks are often the realm of the information architect. In the next chapter, we will describe techniques to get an in-depth understanding of your target audience.

## Learning more...

Especially in the early phases of a project, an information architect often needs to know a little bit about project management. *Web Project Management* by Ashley Friedlein is an excellent manual if you want to pick up some tips on this subject. *The Springboard* by Stephen Denning is great if you need to bring change to an organization—and what information architect doesn't?

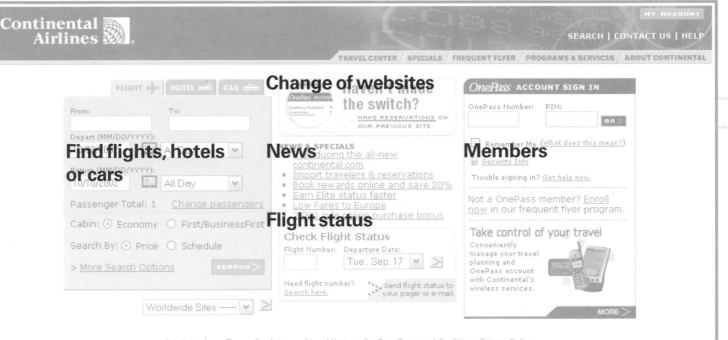

**www. CONTINENTAL.COM**
**Continental Airlines also sells hotel**
**reservations and rental cars, has just had a**
**change in websites, and has the largest**
**section devoted to members.**

# Case study: State of Georgia Online Encyclopedia
## Yet to be published

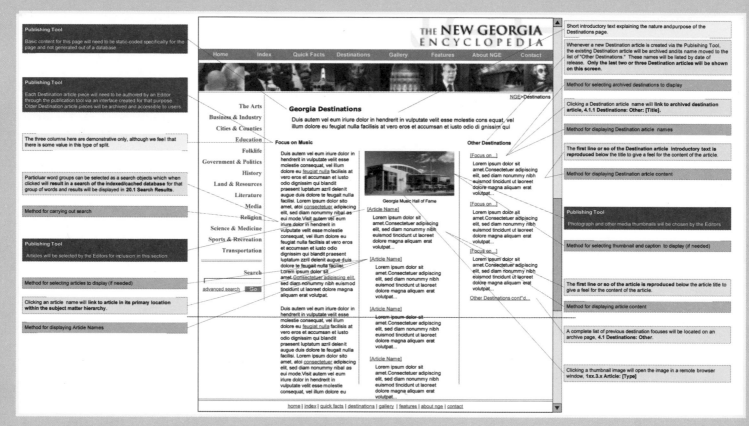

**WEBSITE TEMPLATE**
**The website template shows the different elements on the page and explains their function and the functionality behind them.**

*Understanding the target audience is crucial to the design of the information architecture*

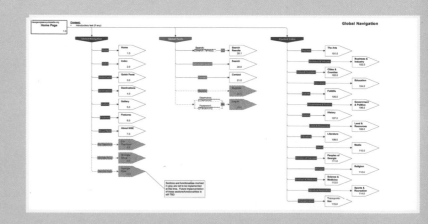

In 2001, the State of Georgia hired Merrillhall (www.merrillhall.com) to design their web-based encyclopedia. They had been publishing encyclopedia content for years, and wanted to make the move to the online medium. An encyclopedia is a challenging project for an information architect: it consists of large amounts of information that can be accessed in many ways. Navigation becomes really important in projects like this.

The New Georgia Encyclopedia is an ambitious project that was first discussed in 1998. It is unusual in that the information architecture of the encyclopedia was designed for the web and for print. It will actually be online before going into print. This makes it the nation's first state encyclopedia conceived at the outset as an online enterprise. The encyclopedia is limited to a single state—Georgia.

## Keep focused on business goals and user goals

Tal Herman served as the lead information architect on the project: "As an IA, it was part of my job to walk the client down the path of understanding designing for a web medium, keeping them focused on two aspects of the design: what they wanted to accomplish, and who they were trying to accomplish this for. Business goals and user goals." The client's experience was almost wholly rooted in another technological medium—the codex (which is a book to you and me)—and they were unused to thinking in terms of either the constraints or the opportunities offered by the web. Tal's job was to educate them about the possibilities of the web, while learning from their experience with books.

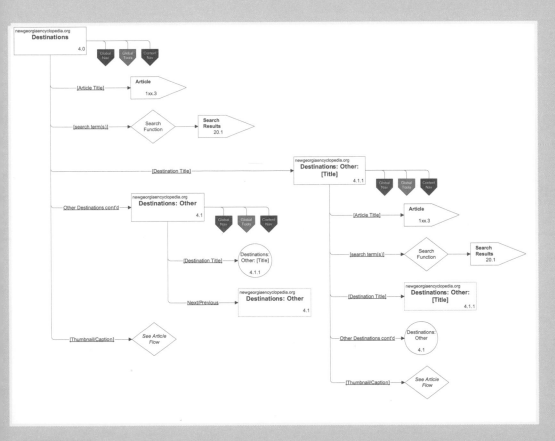

**WEBSITE DIAGRAMS**
These diagrams outline the structure and functionality of the website.

### Share knowledge

The information architect is often the mediator between the knowledge of the client and the knowledge of the team building the solution. This client had a tremendous amount of knowledge and understanding relevant to knowledge transfer and organization in the codex medium. Web designers have a tremendous amount of knowledge about organizing and presenting information in a digital context. Tal recounts: "The client gave us direction based upon their knowledge of the book and we were able to help them translate that into a digital product." This situation is typical in information architecture.

### Understand the target audience

An understanding of the target audience is crucial to the design of a website. Who will use it? What do they want to do? One example in this project was the unexpected importance of counties (a county is larger than a city but smaller than a state). In Georgia (USA), counties are a very important social and organizational unit, often more important than the towns and cities located within them.  Unlike in, say, California, people in Georgia know what county they live in and often something about its history. Because of this, the interface was designed so people could use this knowledge. Without a good understanding of the target audience, details like this are often ignored, resulting in a website that just doesn't feel right.

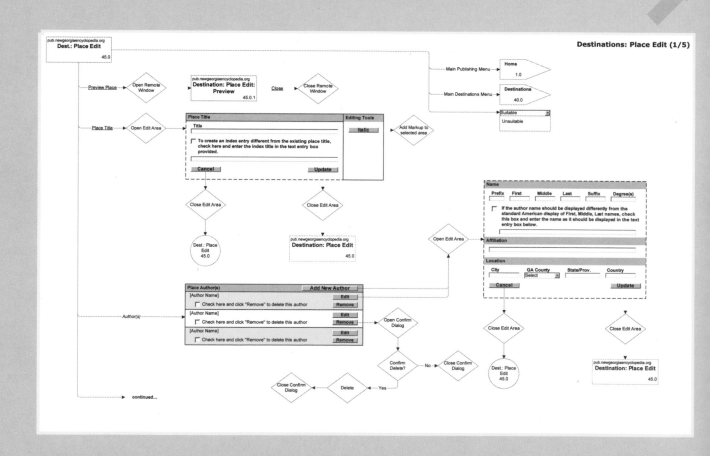

*Keep the client focused on two aspects of the design: what they want to accomplish, and who they are trying to accomplish this for. Business goals and user goals*

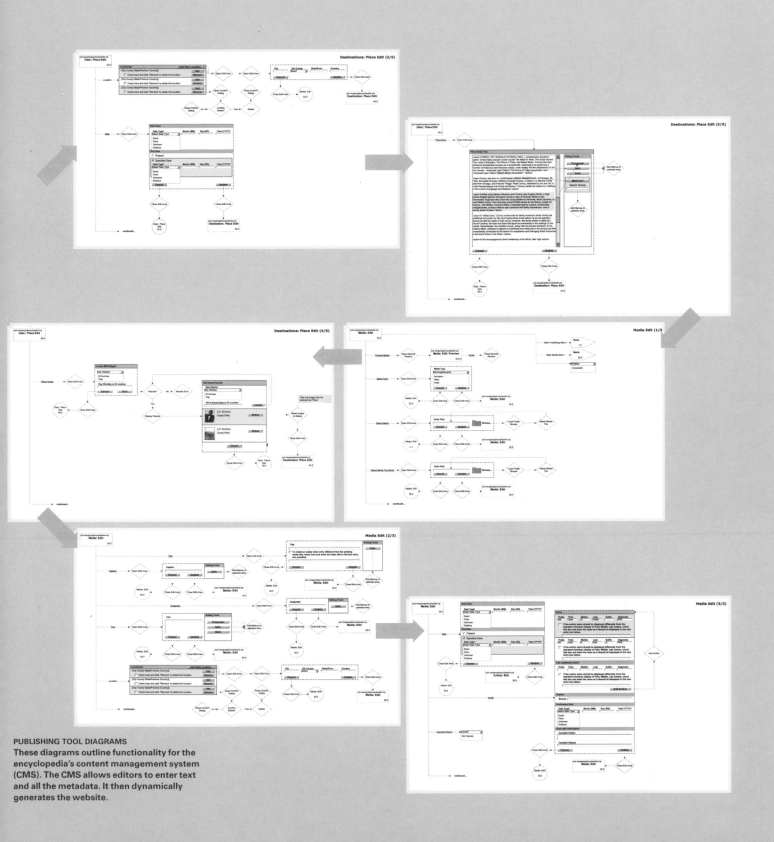

PUBLISHING TOOL DIAGRAMS
These diagrams outline functionality for the
encyclopedia's content management system
(CMS). The CMS allows editors to enter text
and all the metadata. It then dynamically
generates the website.

# Audience research

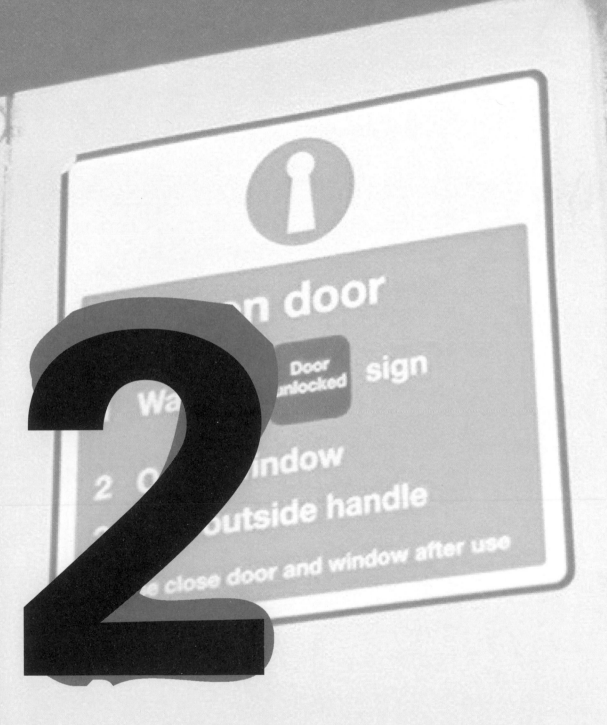

A common mistake when designing a website is to assume that the people who will use it are just like you. Humans naturally assume that other people are like themselves. The goal of researching your audience is to let you step into the shoes of the real users of your website.

Even though this research chapter is one of the longest in the book, don't get the impression that every design decision you make should be based on research. Experience and common sense are even more powerful allies. Doing research gives you insight into how other people use the web, and helps hone your instincts for what will work and what won't. Research creates experience. Experience means you can make informed decisions.

Research will make your life easier, not harder. Remember all those times you have had "which-features-would-be-more-useful" or "how-should-we-implement-this" type discussions? Highly paid teams spend hours arguing about how things should be done, and the arguments are based on little more than personal preference. Having a few research techniques up your sleeve will allow you to find an answer to those questions based on real data, not personal preferences. Doing research is quicker and more cost-effective than going through endless discussions in which not the best argument but the strongest personality usually wins, resulting in the wrong design decision being made for the wrong reason.

## First-time researcher

Audience research just means asking yourself some questions about your audience—something all designers do—and trying to find real answers to those questions. There are plenty of questions that influence design: What is the first thing people want to do on the homepage? What are the three things we want to make really easy for people to do on the website? What percentage of our audience has Flash installed? Answering them from experience is good. Answering them with research is better.

It is easy to build some formal research into a project for the first time. When you ask yourself who your audience is and who you are designing this website for, have a look at the research techniques in this chapter and pick one. You don't have to set up a huge research plan; just spend a few hours on it. You will always learn something interesting, and before you know it you will be doing research for every website you build.

*Humans naturally assume that other people are like themselves*

## Asking the right questions

To do research, you first have to decide what questions you want to answer. Asking good questions is just as important as coming up with answers: answers close the mind, questions open it. When you think you know the answer, you stop looking. Try to answer the wrong question and you are wasting valuable research budget. Focus on formulating the right question first.

The user research questions relevant to web development tend to fall into one of these categories:

• Who is my audience?

• What are their goals?

• What are the best ways for them to achieve their goals?

Generic questions like these should be asked at the start of building of any website: what exactly will people try to do on the website? How will they do it? But websites are more often redesigned than built from scratch. In those cases, the questions to answer tend to be more practical.

To the right are some typical practical research questions. You don't ask the website's users directly—you find ways to answer them by talking to the client about their users. Sometimes these questions are given to you by the client; sometimes you have to think them up yourself.

*Doing research is quicker and more cost-effective than going through endless discussions*

"We're starting a project this fall for a FTSE 100 company that won't go ahead until research is completed outlining the direction that it should take this year. We suggested researching their audience last year and it worked so well that they want to do it again, ensuring that we're still moving in the right direction. Nothing replaces experience. However, some old-fashioned research helps to solidify your hypotheses almost every time. We've never found research to be a waste."
**Jared Folkmann, Information Architect**

"On one project, I called local hotels and set up 15-minute interviews with the concierge at each. It didn't take up any more of the budget than sitting at my desk guessing either, and was much more valuable."
**Garrick Van Buren, Information Architect**

"I almost always do some user research, and usually commit a good proportion of my resources to it. When I have had to do without, I worry that I have made the wrong assumptions about the users and may be designing something that they cannot use."
**Donna Maurer, Information Architect**

**Question:** "We are considering adding a certain piece of new functionality to our website, but is it worth the expense?"

First, find out what business goals this new functionality is trying to support—why does the client want it? Talk to the client: what positive effect do they expect this functionality to have? More people visiting the site? More sales? Try to put numbers on it. You can easily calculate the expected profit (actual profit is usually lower) against the expected cost (actual cost is usually higher), and decide if it is worth building.

Next, talk to users and find out if the new functionality addresses a real user goal. Often clients imagine users are having certain problems, when the real problems lie somewhere else. Building functionality to address the wrong problems is a waste of money. Use interviews or other research techniques described in this chapter to find out if this functionality addresses real user problems, and, if not, what the real user problems are.

**Question:** "How can we get more people to join our mailing list?"

Again, find out what the real question is first. Does the client want to get more people coming to the website through this mailing list? Or sell more advertising on the mailing list? That is your business goal.

Next, talk to users and observe them signing up. This way, you can identify obstacles to signing up, whether they are on the sign-up page or in the user's head. A usability test (explained later in this chapter) will show if the subscription page is hard to use—a surprisingly large number of subscription pages are. Interviews can uncover further confusion that users may experience, or problems with the perception of the mailing list.

**Question:** "We have lots of technical support documents—how can we best put them on the web?"

Let's assume the client has no existing website—so there is nothing up there to test. You need to find out how users will want to use these documents. Will they look for documents by product name, product identifier, or problem category? Chapter 3, page 77, discusses how to design an appropriate information architecture. You can start by examining the documents. Then interview customer support personnel. What are the top 10 needs of people contacting them?

As you can see from these example questions, the first thing is to uncover the truth behind the question. Work on the question before you start working on the answer. You will usually end up with more than one research question.

*Research creates experience*

*Answers close the mind, questions open it*

*Work on the question before you start working on the answer*

# Designing and selling a research plan

Before you set out to do research, design a research plan. It will list the research questions you are trying to answer, the methodologies you will use, and how long you expect this to take you. It doesn't have to be final—often you will change your research plan as you go— but it should give a good indication of what you are planning to do.

A research plan also gives you a good overview of your assumptions: you may have expected to hear A and B, but when doing the research people talked about A and C, and nobody even mentioned B. Finding out things you didn't foresee is extremely valuable, and a central reason for doing research. The best thing about research is the surprises. A typical research plan looks something like this:

**Typical research plan**

Research goals:
- Find out what people in our (previously defined) target audience want from our financial services website.
- Definition of motivation and tasks:
     We expect the main tasks of our users to be:
     -Research and compare different options.
     -Keep track of their investments and know when they should take some form of action.

     We expect the main psychological drivers of our users to be:
     -A need to feel they can trust the website.
     -A need for comprehensive information.

Research methods:
- We will use 10 in-depth one-on-one interviews, combined with data analysis with key members of the team. Results will be written in a report.

Estimated timeline:
- Prepare interview guide: 4 hours.
- Find people within our target audience to interview and arrange interviews: 4 hours (spread out over a week).
- Five initial interviews at home of interviewee.
     For each interview:
     -2 hours per interview, plus 2 hours travel.
     -Transcribing interview (using software): 1 hour.
     -Initial analysis and refocusing of interview guide: 1 hour.
     -Data analysis and writing final report: 16 hours.

Presenting report:
- To client team: 1 hour.
- To internal team: 1 hour.

The research plan is often used to sell the research to the client. Add a motivation for doing the research by describing the deliverables and expected outcome of the research. Here is an example:

**Example research motivation**

Expected outcome:
A detailed understanding of the motivations and tasks of the target audience of this website will lead directly to better decisions on features and information architecture of the website, since these decisions will be based on real data, and not personal preferences or best guesses. We expect this research to be useful throughout the life of the website.

We will provide:
- An actionable report, listing users' motivations and tasks, ordered by user group (as defined in earlier research), which will feed directly into decisions about the current and future information architecture of the website.

- A data analysis exercise for the entire team to help focus the team on the users' needs. This will enable a discussion of features and functionality based on real user data, not just personal opinions.

"On an e-business project, the client said there was no need for user research because they knew everything about their potential users. I knew we needed to explore users and their needs. Instead of telling the client that we had to do research, I asked a series of probing questions about the users. When no one could satisfactorily answer questions like 'Why would a user choose to use this application instead of their current process?' or 'What would increase the frequency of use?' the client suggested that we research the answers. Helping the client realize the need for user research is much more effective than telling them it needs to be done. When the client suggests the task, they are more generous in allocating resources for it."
**Kathy Marshak, Senior Consultant for IconMedialab**

# Why client market research isn't enough

Clients often believe the market research they have done (and usually paid a lot of money for) should be enough for you to work with. It rarely is. Typical market research results look like this:

### Example of client market research

"28 to 32-year-old, non-married women with high-paying jobs, living in the city, are likely to use this website. 86.2% indicated they would visit 'at least once a week', and over two thirds (77.3%) said they would recommend it to their friends. The 'order the same item weekly' feature was rated highest amongst the features we proposed."

Explain to your client that the market research is for advertising purposes, and is all about attitudes and demographics. Information architecture user research is meant to make sure the website actually works well and is easy to use, and deals with goals and tasks. Typically, the results look more like this:

### Information architecture research

"Our core audience consists of working mothers with high-paying jobs. Their main reason for using our website is convenience and saving time. The main potential problem that would prevent usage of the site is reliability/trust.

'If the packages get here on time I don't mind paying a bit more' Typical interviewee.

Tasks the website should support are (in order of importance):

1. Find a known item and buy it. Little comparison shopping and little searching for new items.

2. Order the same or similar items on a (bi-)weekly basis.

3. Get personal support if something goes wrong (users expect high levels of support)."

**Planning time for your research**

When planning time for your research, allow enough time for analysis and transcribing. Don't plan four full days of consecutive full-on research either: plan half a day of analysis for each day of research, so you can refine your research questions.

**Do an initial research exercise**

When planning research that will take over a week, do an initial data-gathering exercise or two before finalizing the plan. It will help you estimate the amount of time you'll need, and the specific challenges you might encounter.

**Don't sell research as a separate step**

Unless you have a particularly enlightened client, or have a really large research project, just work the time for it in the normal schedule. If you separate it out as an individual step it looks like something that can be removed.

**A little research can go a long way**

Don't feel like you have to do a two-week-long research project in order to get valuable results. A few hours spent on research can fit into almost any schedule, and they will always pay off.

"Once we were examining the site visitor statistics of a website, which showed that for every 100 visits to the newsletter sign-up page, only 25 resulted in a sign-up. It turned out that people were going to the sign-up page to gather more information about the magazine subscription. We moved some information off that page, made it prominent where it was meant to be, and although total visits to the newsletter sign-up went down, actual sign-ups increased.

Also, more magazine subscriptions occurred, indicating that, previously, some potential subscribers were declining because they couldn't find that bit of extra detail that was hidden on an inappropriate page."
**Eric Scheid, Information Architect for Ironclad Networks**

# Three easy research methods

Research methods are techniques for gathering information. It's how you do research. Later in this chapter, in "Three research deliverables," we'll explain how to use this information, but first you must gather it, by using one of these techniques:

• **Interviews**
These are a great way to find out how people think about things.

• **Observation with contextual inquiry**
This lets you find out how people actually do things—which is different from what they think about them.

• **Usability testing**
This is a good way to find out whether a page is easy to use, and, if not, what the problem is.

These methods are some of the most powerful ways to gather data relevant to information architects. Try them all, so you know how they work. Then you can pick the most useful one whenever you need to find out something about your audience.

### Interviews

Interviews are a great way to find out what your audience's goals, priorities, and problems are. These are often not what you expect, and the best way to find out is to ask them. The most useful type of interviews for audience research is the one-on-one interview: you spend an hour or so talking in-depth with one person, and repeat this with other interviewees until you have enough information.

It is always best to interview people who would naturally be interested in your website. If you are building a website for young parents, find some young parents. If you sell books, get people who read lots of books. You can try finding these people yourself (friends of friends are good), or have a company select them for you—which can be expensive. Avoid using friends or colleagues, as they will be too eager to please you with their answers. Most people like being interviewed: it isn't every day that someone listens with complete interest to your opinions for a full hour.

When interviewing, get people to talk freely about their attitudes and motivations, while keeping focused on what you want to find out. Let people wander off to get unexpected insights, but bring them back on track when they start discussing things unrelated to your research. Ask open-ended, practical questions that deal with their personal experiences.

*If you want to find out about their behavior, observe people.*
*If you want to find out about their attitudes and beliefs, interview them*

**Avoid focus groups**

Focus groups are a well-known type of interview where marketing people talk to groups of users. Your client may want you to use focus groups as a research technique. They aren't very useful when building websites, however, and are best avoided.

"I was talking to users about their experiences with a website. One of them told me that it was hard to read particular information. I couldn't understand the problem from this description, so I said, 'Show me.' He opened his favorites in the left-hand side of the browser window, opened the website and eventually opened a PDF file. By the time he got to the PDF file, he had three sets of navigators on the left (favorites, website navigation, and the PDF navigator)—there was hardly any room for the content! I would not have understood the problem without watching what he did."
**Donna Maurer, Information Architect**

**Bad question:** "Is this a useful feature?"
Most people aren't web designers; they can't tell you how to build your website.
**Good question:** "Would you use this feature this week in your work?" (practical!)

 **Bad question:** "What should go on the homepage?"
You are the web designer, not them.
**Good question:** "When you visit a website like this, what is the first thing you want to do or know?"

**Bad question:** "How do you currently use the site?"
Actually, this question isn't that bad. But people are famously bad at self-reporting. If you want to know how somebody does something, ask them to show you.
**Better question:** "Can you show me how you currently use the site?"

Beware of the please-the-interviewer syndrome. Most interviewees will unconsciously try to say what they think you want to hear. Avoid this by keeping the focus on their practical experience.

Allowing your decisions to be driven by user requests is bad design methodology, because people tend not to know or articulate what they want without direction, even though they will happily tell you if you ask them. Instead, you should try to uncover their goals and tasks, and then decide yourself how the website can best serve those, and whether it fits in with your business goals.

**BAD INTERVIEW TOPICS: USING INTERVIEWS LIKE THIS IS BAD METHODOLOGY...**

Here are a few typical interview approaches in an information architecture context:

**Research question:** "What do people like and dislike about the competition's website?"
**Interview approach:** Ask people who already use these websites to walk you through a competitor's website and explain what they like and what they don't like. You should do this on a computer so they can show you the website. Seeing it will remind them of more things to tell you. Keep asking them how elements of the website affect what they are trying to do.

**Research question:** "Which features should we implement first?"
**Interview approach:** Do not ask people which features they like best. People are notoriously bad at answering this type of question. Instead, interview them about the problems they currently encounter. The features that address those problems best should be implemented.

**Research question:** "How should we organize our website?"
**Interview approach:** Ask people to describe the tasks they will be fulfilling on the website in their own words, and note down what words and concepts they use. This will give you an indication of how they think about these tasks; base your organization on this.

(See Chapter 3, page 77, for more information on organization.)

It is easy to forget a topic while doing an interview, so write yourself an interview guide—a list of questions or topics you want to discuss.

When setting up interviews, there are a few practical things to keep in mind. Write a consent form explaining why you are doing the interviews, and that the interviewee has the right to stop at any time. Always try to pay your interviewees a small sum for expenses. Audiotape the interview—it makes it easier to pull out relevant quotes later on, and it looks professional. You can make notes as well, but try not to let it interfere with the interview. You should be focused on listening, not on making notes. Transcribing the interview (writing it out) can be useful for later analysis, but takes a lot of time—most people don't bother.

**Interview preparation checklist:**

✔ Spend time on a good research question.

✔ Tape recorder, empty tapes and back-up batteries.

✔ Interview guide with topics you want to cover.

✔ Enough copies of interview consent forms.

✔ Did you plan enough time for data analysis between interviews?

"I was doing one-on-one interviews in the participants' setting and took our visual designer along for the trip. The people we were talking to use the internet as part of their job—usually particular sites to perform tasks. In the course of our conversation, one woman said, 'I have two internets—Netscape Navigator and Yahoo.' We laughed about this later, but were reminded: 'This is who we are designing for.' Having seen this in person was much more effective than just reporting back—that's why I like taking members of the team to do research. The designer is still telling this story as a reminder of our target audience."
**Katie Ware, Information Architect**

**How much research is enough?**

When do you know you've done enough research? When you see a pattern emerging that can inform design. When you can make confident design decisions. Once you start hearing or observing the same things again and again you have probably reached a plateau in your research: either stop or go do some analysis and come up with more research questions. Research on five people is often enough—although it depends on the research method. Research done with only one person is almost always unreliable.

### Observation with contextual inquiry

Observation is the best way to find out how people actually do things. Contextual inquiry is a specific technique that combines observation with interviews. It leads to detailed insights about how people do complex things like buying a car, choosing a loan, or staying in touch with their fly-fishing buddies. Once you know exactly how people do those things, what their problems and specific needs are, you can support those tasks on your website.

The "contextual" part is crucial—it means that you have to go to where people are currently doing these tasks. Yes, get out of your office. Observe people where and when they do things for real: usually at home or at work.

Contextual inquiry tends to take time—the time for transportation alone will eat up lots of budget. A typical contextual inquiry exercise will take at least a week: a day for planning and finding people, two and a half days of observation and interviews, and a day and a half of analysis.

Let's look at an example: say we are building a website to help people manage their personal finances: bank accounts, bills, investments, and so on. Contextual inquiry can help us to answer questions like: What are the main problems people have when dealing with their personal finances? What (if any) are the stages people go through when dealing with personal finances? Do married people do this differently than single people? And so on.

To do contextual inquiry, go and observe people dealing with their finances in their natural environment: probably at home. Find some people in your target audience, and explain to them you are doing research for a website that wants to help people manage their finances. Ask them when they normally do their finances, and ask if you can come over and observe them doing this.

People often don't understand what you're trying to do when you ask to observe them. They might think they're being tested, or that you're going to report on how well they do to their boss. Sometimes they think you are there to explain to them how they should do things, and they feel angry about that.

**CONTEXTUAL INQUIRY**

It's your responsibility as a researcher (did I mention you're a researcher now?) to make them feel good about the process. One way to explain this is to explain the relationship as a master-apprentice relationship. They are the master and you are the apprentice: you want to learn how they do things by observing them in action.

Researching people is fun, but you should always be aware of possible ethical implications and think about the feelings of the people you are researching:

• They might feel obliged to answer you.

• They might feel intimidated by you.

• They might worry about what the things they said will be used for.

To allay these fears you should:

• Clearly explain to them what the research will be used for.

• Clearly explain to them that they can stop at any time during the research if they feel uncomfortable for any reason.

• Have them sign a consent form that outlines their rights before starting. An example consent form can be found on our website ⊟ .

Also, make sure you emphasize that you're not testing them— you're there to learn how they do these tasks. Observe them doing what they do, and ask them questions about it when something is not clear: "Why are you doing that?" "Do you usually do it like this?" Take a notebook for the observation, a camera (a cheap one will do) and something to record interviews with.

Contextual inquiry as a technique is such fun that it is easy to forget to spend time doing analysis: i.e. going over your notes and thinking about what it all means. When doing analysis, try to identify goals, motivations, and tasks, and look for insights into how your website can better support these.

Contextual inquiry is a very powerful technique in really understanding the needs, goals, and tasks of your target audience. It can lead to insights into the hidden goals and needs of your audience that are currently not being addressed by you or the competition.

---

**Contextual analysis planning checklist**

✔ Make sure you make the situation as real as possible: use people who do the tasks you want to study for real. Spend enough time finding the right people to study.

✔ Plan to study at least four different people, usually more.

✔ Study groups of people (families, groups of friends) instead of individuals if appropriate.

✔ Plan at least half a day of data analysis for each day of data gathering.

✔ Plan a data presentation meeting where you present the data, not just the conclusions, to the team. Plan at least half a day to prepare this.

---

*Observe people in their natural environment*

---

**Contextual inquiry: keep it real**

When doing contextual inquiry, you are trying to observe real-life behavior. Sometimes people act differently just because you are observing them. When in doubt, ask if they would normally do it like this.

The reason why this technique of observing people works so well is that what people say they do, and what they actually do is often very different. So don't ask them how they manage their finances (try it—you will get some really boring answers); ask them if you can observe them for a few hours actually doing their finances.

After completing the observation is a good time to do an interview. Thank them for their time, and take an hour or so to go over your observations together (this is called participant confirmation), and talk more about what you observed. Take some pictures— they will be useful when giving presentations to your colleagues or client.

THE FOLLOW-UP INTERVIEW: THIS CAN UNCOVER MORE USEFUL INFORMATION...

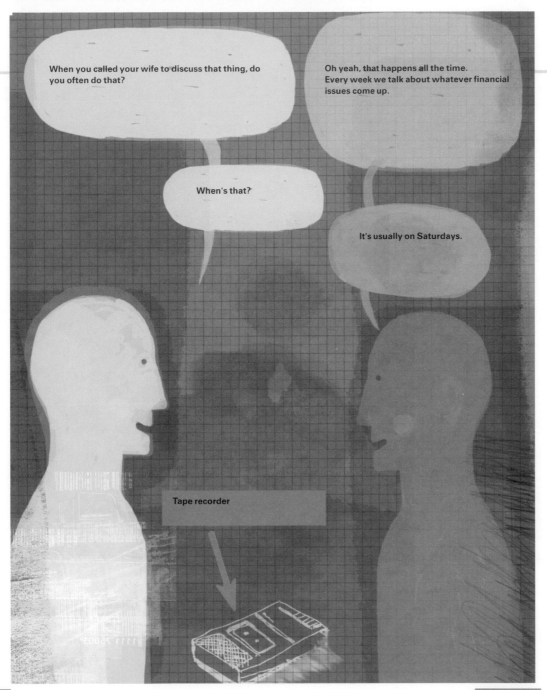

**Finding test participants**

In contextual inquiry, it's important to study people doing the tasks you want to study for real, not pretending to do them. Demographics (age, occupation) don't matter as much as finding people who do the tasks you want to do research on.

Market research firms can help you find participants, but are usually not experienced in finding the type of people you need, so explain to them that you are not so much looking for demographics, but for people who do certain tasks.

**Go through your notes every night**

If you're doing contextual inquiry for more than one day, ensure you go through your notes every evening, and make additional notes. It's amazing how much detail you forget if you leave your notes for a few days.

**3**

## Usability testing

Usability testing determines how easy it is to use a website (or any design—you could test a cup to find out if it was easy to use). It is another observation technique whereby you give someone a task to perform ("order a catalogue"), and observe them doing it. The people doing the test are asked to "think out loud" while using the website; that is, to talk about what they are doing. As an observer, you don't talk, you just take notes.

Usability testing is an extremely powerful way to find out what is wrong with a website, what works and what doesn't. It's fast too—a quick usability test can be finished within 20 minutes.

Setting up a usability test is easy:

- Decide on what you want to test: the entire website or a certain piece of functionality?

- Write down the task(s) you will give people. For example: "Visit this website, have a look around and become a member," or: "Look for a dress on this website and buy it."

- Find people to test. They don't really have to fit your target audience closely, although it is better if they do. Don't use people in your team who have worked on the website.

A quick test of a certain webpage can be done with some people in the office and take only 20 minutes. In-depth testing of a website is usually done with five or more people, spending one hour with each.

When doing the actual tests, make sure you explain to people that you are not testing them, but the website. People understandably get nervous when they think they are being tested. Then explain to them you won't be saying anything, but that you'd like them to vocalize their thoughts. Tell them you want to hear about their experience with the website: their expectations (when it did or didn't work as expected); their feelings (satisfied, angry, frustrated); and why they are doing certain things. Expectations are really important. Also mention that they can ask you any question they want, but that you will answer them afterwards, rather than during the test. Tell them to imagine you are not there.

Then give them a task and just observe. Try not to talk, apart from occasionally saying things like "What do you mean by that?" or "Keep talking." This is often the hardest thing to do for first-time testers. It's really frustrating when you see someone trying to find a button (like "shopping basket") that is right in front of them—you're tempted to prompt them.

Often people don't start thinking out loud straight away when looking at the first page, so say something like: "Please keep talking out loud." Once people get started, just take notes. After the test is finished, discuss your notes with them to make sure you didn't misinterpret anything.

If you do this with a few people, and then work through your notes, you should end up with a clear list of usability problems. It's not always necessary to write up the results of a usability test, but if you do, make sure you plan at least one day of analysis and writing per day of testing.

**Increasing motivation with real money**

Testing is often done on a beta version of a website where everything works except for the credit card part. However, when testing an existing e-commerce website, you could give people a real credit card and tell them they can keep whatever they buy (up to a certain amount). This will make your test more realistic, as the users will be motivated.

**Everyone should do usability testing**

You don't have to be an expert with a degree in human-computer interaction to do a usability test. On the contrary, it's important that everyone in the team learns how to do them. Try one out with a co-worker—remember to observe and not to interrupt them, and don't draw conclusions from observing just one person. You will be surprised at how much you learn.

**Invite a team member to your usability test**

Invite a designer, programmer, or anyone on your team to join the test. It's a great way to increase the value of the tests, and increase awareness of usability issues in your team. Tell them it's fun, but they have to be quiet. Give them a notebook, and discuss the test afterwards with them. It's cheaper than sending them to an expensive usability conference, and often more effective in creating awareness. Don't invite the entire team all at once though; get only one or two additional observers for each session. If you have a video camera you can set it up so people can follow the test from outside the room.

**REAL-LIFE INFORMATION ARCHITECTURE**
Older trains still in use in the UK were not designed for today's speed of travel, resulting in unusual real-life information architecture. The sign on the door instructs passengers to wait for the train to stop before opening the window to release the door externally. This prevents the left-hinged doors flying violently open in the moving train's airstream if prematurely opened from the inside.

*It's important that everyone in the team learns how to do usability testing*

**Usability testing day checklist:**

✔ Do you have a working computer in a quiet room? Is everything set up?

✔ Did you send a confirmation email?

✔ Is someone taking care of the participants as they come in?

✔ Do you have plenty of consent forms printed out for them to sign?

✔ If you're using a tape recorder or videotape, did you test them out and do you have plenty of blank tapes and batteries?

✔ Do you have a written list of things to tell the participants before starting the test?

✔ Did you plan enough time for writing up the results?

✔ Did you prepare clear tasks to give them, including some back-up tasks if they fail the first task?

### Which method to use?

Which research method should you use? It depends on what you are trying to find out.

**Interviews** are a good way to find out what people want from a website. Interviews can help answer questions like: "How do people use the internet to look for jobs?" or "What elements of the intranet do people find most useful?" They don't take too much time and are easy to organize.

**Observation with contextual inquiry** gives you more detailed insights in how people do things. It is often used to determine strategic questions related to complex functionality, like "What functionality should we implement?" or "How can we better support the needs of our HR department?" It takes time though, and planning.

**Usability testing** is the bread and butter of research techniques. It can answer practical questions like: Why is this page hard to use? Where should that button go? A quick usability test can be finished in 20 minutes. Everyone on the team making interface decisions (designers, information architects, programmers) should learn how to do usability testing.

**SETTING UP THE USABILITY TEST**

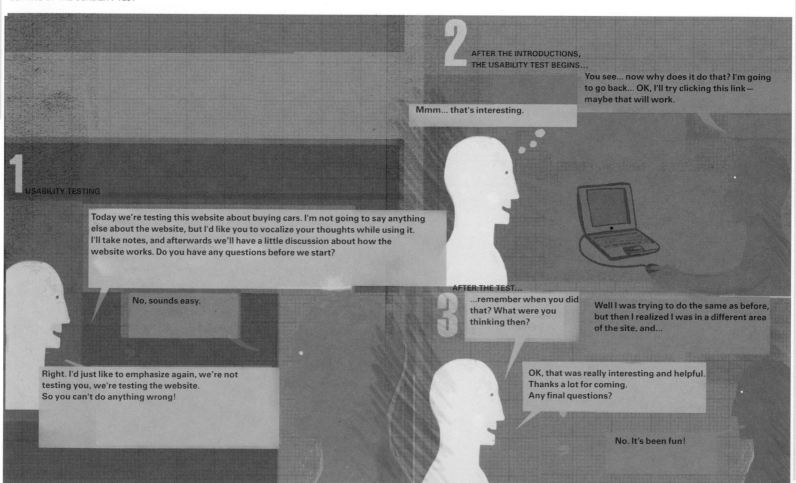

# Analyzing your research

Analysis means turning your data (the interviews and observations) into answers to your research questions. Sometimes it means changing your questions into better questions. Analysis is not something you do after you have concluded all the research; it starts while doing research. After the first few interviews, review them to find patterns, then focus on those in subsequent interviews. After the first round of observation, review your notes and look for patterns that will influence design.

When you start analyzing the information you have gathered with your research, review your notes and try to find patterns. Don't base conclusions on something that one person did; base them on things that crop up again and again. Look out for surprises: things that people did or said that you didn't expect. These often contain the most valuable insights. If people are behaving exactly as you thought they would, look harder—or end the research, as you aren't learning anything new.

One really useful technique for doing analysis is to write all your ideas on cards and organize them—you might have learned this technique in school for writing papers. It's called card sorting. If you want to impress people you can call it affinity diagramming (which just means putting similar things together). To do card sorting, identify quotes, concepts, and ideas that you have encountered in your research, and write them down on small cards or sticky notes. Sticky notes, by the way, are the information architect's best friend.

Put them on a big table or hang them on a wall (walls are an information architect's second-best friend)—and put the ones that seem to go together, well, together. Then give these groups of things names, like "trust" or "control" as in the example over the page. Combine quotes and concepts into ideas that can ultimately influence design. If two cards are really about the same concept, combine them.

The result of a card-sorting exercise is a number of issues you discovered in the research. This will be the basis of your answers to the questions. Note that sometimes card sorting is used to discover what categories should go on your website—in this case you get users to do the card sorting to find out how they categorize things. Chapter 3, page 77, explains how.

Overleaf is an example of how a card-sorting exercise with interview data could go.

*Analysis means turning your data into answers to your research questions*

**Step 1:**
Highlight interesting concepts and quotes in the interview transcript.

**Q:** "What is your main concern when trying out your bank's online service?"

**A:** "Well, I'd be worried about losing control over my money. I mean, I know it is silly, but you never know what they'll do—maybe they'd take even more money? Are there hidden charges for using this kind of technology rather than just going into your local branch? It's like, how do I know if I can trust them? Anyone can put up a website… I've heard horror stories about fraud online and would worry about the security—I mean, if I enter all my account details, how do I know that some hacker won't have immediate access to my account?

Also, security aside, I'd want to know how quickly any transactions I made online would be acknowledged by my bank—if I transferred money from my savings account into my current account to avoid going overdrawn, for example, can I be sure that the technology is dependable and that this transfer will be honored so that I don't incur any charges? My main concern here would be that I wouldn't have any paper record of my transactions."

**Step 2:**
Write the quotes and concepts on cards.

" Anyone can put up a website"

"Trust my bank's website"

"Losing control over my money"

"Maybe they take even more money?"

"No paper record of my transactions"

# 3

**Step 3:**
Organize the cards into groups around higher-level concepts.

# 4

**Step 4:**
These concepts lead to practical conclusions and design recommendations, like the following:

## Trust

## Control

**Conclusions from audience research and design recommendations**

The main issues users have when wanting to try out our service are about trust and control. They worry whether they can trust us, and whether they will retain control over their money.

We recommend addressing these issues in the design of the website as follows:

[outline design recommendations here...]

**"Trust my bank's website"**

**"Losing control over my money"**

**"Anyone can put up a website"**

**"Maybe they take even more money?"**

**"No paper record of my transactions"**

# Three research deliverables

The three research methods just described over the last few pages are ways of collecting information. Now we will describe what you can do with that data. The deliverables described in the following section aren't used just because they are cool. Think of them as design tools that can support the design process.

- **Audience analysis**
  This is a description of your audience, divided into categories.

- **Personas**
  These are short descriptions of archetypical people of your audience.

- **Scenarios**
  These are short stories describing how people may use the website.

*Think of research methods as design tools that can support the design process*

### Audience analysis

An audience analysis is a document that provides a breakdown and analysis of your audience that helps the team to make design decisions. It is used by the entire design team to better understand who they are designing for. For example, it helps to start from an audience analysis when brainstorming on content and features for the website.

A typical audience analysis presents a few types of audiences, specific information about them, and their tasks and goals. You can also indicate the importance of the audience. Here's an example:

**Example of audience analysis**

The target audience of our website consists of customers (93%), investors (1%), press (2%) and employees (4%).

Customers visit the website mainly because they want technical support (TC customers—60%) or because they are doing research on our products (research customers—40%).

TC customers demand a high level of service. Our research has shown that if they can't find the right support on the website within five minutes they will call the call centre—a cost we want to avoid.

An estimated 75% of TC customers are looking to download updated drivers. The other 25% have diverse tasks: configuration questions, general questions about our products, returning faulty products…

Notice how the analysis doesn't provide solutions; it just describes the goals and needs of the target audience in detail (the above example is just an introduction), in a way that will help us make design decisions (for example: finding drivers should be really easy). An audience analysis can be reused throughout the life of a website. It will often be reused and updated as more research is done.

As with all our research deliverables, an audience analysis is based on a variety of research sources: interviews, usability tests, traffic logs of an existing website, market research, and so on.

The most important element of doing audience analysis is to share the results with the team, so don't just write a document and file it—organize a meeting with the team, so they can get familiar with the audience.

## Personas

Personas are descriptions of archetypical examples of your target audience. You can refer to them in design discussions: "This solution wouldn't work for Bob" (where Bob is a persona). Personas help you to talk and think about your target audience as real people.

Personas should used by the entire team throughout the development of the website. They excel at describing motivation and goals for specific parts of the target audience. They are usually combined with scenarios, and together these two form a powerful tool for your design process.

**VISUALIZING PERSONAS**

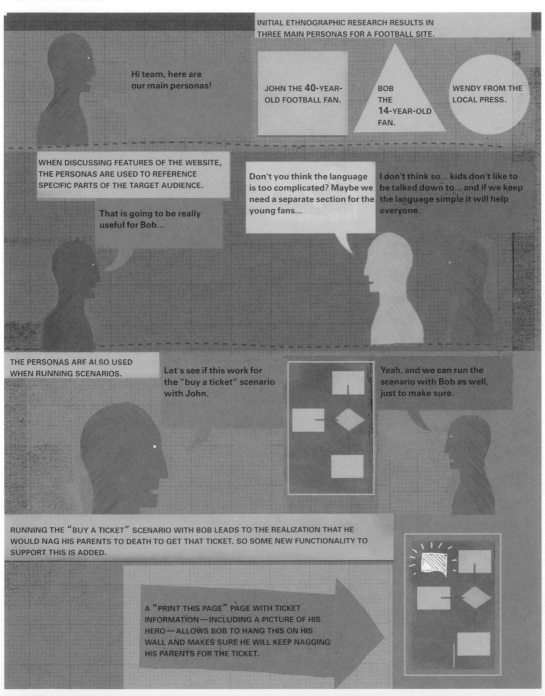

Using personas creates definitions of type and this encourages empathy as you imagine your users as real people. This helps you to design better websites. When making a design decision, it helps to consider whether your mom would like it this way (that is, if your mom is in the target audience). Why? Because you like your mom. You wouldn't develop a website she would find frustrating to use, would you?

Of course, your mom isn't always a good example of the target audience—that's why we do research and come up with a small set of different personas—usually fewer than five. If you end up with more than five personas, you can probably combine two into one. Each persona represents a typical part of your audience with different needs. Personas aren't descriptions of real people or even job descriptions. Instead, they describe behavior patterns. Note that your personas are design tools; often they are different from your marketing or sales targets.

When designing personas, focus on goals. What do they want out of this website? What do they need to do? A good goal is a specific, practical thing that they want to get out of the website. Write a one-page description for each persona, containing:

•Their name and a picture; you can use pictures from a magazine to visualise your personas.

•A short but lively description of who they are, including descriptions of skills ("limited internet experience"); attitudes ("doesn't like to waste time"); and constraints ("has no access to broadband internet"). Also add some personal details (marital status, job, hobbies) that make the persona easy to remember.

•Most importantly, make a detailed description of their two to five main goals for the website. Make it detailed ("wants to share pictures online with her family, who are all over the country, especially pictures of her kids").

Right is an example of a persona for a non-profit website that helps people to manage their personal finances:

**Example persona: Mason**

Typical quote:
"Where can I find trustworthy advice?"

Mason (32) works in a trucking company that just lowered his wage. He's not married, but has a long-term relationship. He has invested his few savings carefully and conservatively (no stock), has little debt, but now he is worried about not having enough money when he retires. He also has this nagging feeling he's not getting enough out of his savings. He is familiar with email and visits a handful of websites about his hobbies regularly (via a dial-up connection). He bought some fishing gear online last month, and that went well.

Mason's goals are:
•To decide if he is currently doing a good job managing his finances.

•To get reliable, trustworthy advice on how to do better, and what steps to take.

•To decide if the web is a good place to get advice or if visiting a local bank or asking friends would be better

•To decide if he is doing a good job managing his finances.

He has already discussed this last point with some friends. One of them recommended our website. Others gave conflicting advice: more stock, less stock, and so on. So he is not sure who to trust. He isn't sure the web is the best place to get reliable advice, but he had good experiences getting advice from websites about his hobbies, so he wants to give it a try. He is mostly worried about ending up on a commercial website that has a double agenda.

"On many recent projects we have found client opinion starting to dictate the direction of the website, often to the detriment of the end user. By using personas we remind everyone in the project team (both client and consultancy) who they are designing the end product for. Sometimes all you need is 'Bob the Student' or 'Samantha the Institutional Investor' to step up and put the project back on track."
**Jared Folkmann, Information Architect**

*Personas describe behavior patterns*

Note how the persona focuses on very specific goals, but doesn't say how the website will work. That comes later. The typical quote sums up the persona.

Once you have finished your personas, you should organize a meeting for the team to become familiar with them. Your goal is to have the team refer to personas in discussions about design decisions: "But that would work for Jenny the secretary." Some information architects make a poster for each persona and hang these on their walls.

When your team isn't familiar with using personas, take time to introduce and discuss them. Much of the value of personas comes from being used by the team, so getting them interested is worth your while.

When introducing personas to a technical team, it may help to compare them to "use cases." These are a way to express requirements that programmers are usually familiar and comfortable with. Explain that personas and scenarios can be refined later in the process into use cases.

When introducing personas to visual designers, ask them to illustrate them and to help you make posters for them. When introducing personas to your client, refer to market research. They will likely be familiar with the value of that. Explain to them that personas are a way to increase the return on investment of your user research, by providing an easy way for everyone in the team to use the results. Also mention that personas can often be reused in future stages, so creating them is an investment that keeps paying off after the first project.

**THINK ABOUT YOUR AUDIENCE AS REAL PEOPLE**

**3**

## Scenarios

Scenarios are little stories that describe how people would ideally use the website. The value of scenarios is that they relate website functions to user goals, which makes it a lot easier to discuss and make the right design decisions. Scenarios are especially useful in combination with personas: the personas describe motivation and goals; the scenarios describe concrete tasks.

Creating scenarios is easy; write a little story (a few paragraphs) that describes how a certain user (a persona) would ideally use the website. Note the word "ideally"; you want to write a successful story that represents a perfect session in which both user and business goals are fulfilled.

Either you will have done some research to base your stories on, or you can use your common sense and make them up. Try to create realistic stories that describe an ideal usage of your website. Think about user goals and business goals when writing scenarios. Don't create one for every possible usage of the site, just the ideal core scenarios.

Here are three example scenarios, imagining how three different personas would use a non-profit website that helps people to manage their personal finances:

### Scenario 1

Persona: Sally

Age: 23

Occupation: Legal clerk

Scenario: Sally is surfing the Net in her lunch break at work. She enters the site via an advert from another website entitled "Make sense of your finances".

On the homepage, there is a link to a "Personal finance wizard", a calculator which allows her to enter her salary and her monthly outgoings. She is then invited to register her personal details on the site so that she won't have to re-enter her details next time. A friend calls for a chat and she is interrupted, so she decides to register later.

### Scenario 2

Persona: Mason

Age: 32

Occupation: Truck driver

It's morning. On his first visit to the website, Mason wants to find out if this website can help him out. When he gets to our homepage, he has already visited three other websites that were recommended to him—he didn't like them, though. His patience is being tested.

The homepage presents some quick reassurance about the impartiality of the website—Mason glances at it. There is a section with articles about figuring out how to manage your finances—the titles seem relevant to him. His attention is drawn to one called, "How are you managing your finances—take the test." He goes to the article, and quickly scans it. It tells him a few things he didn't know—he likes it and looks for more interesting things on this website.

There are links to more in-depth discussions, and a list of similar introductory articles. He goes to the introductory article: "Discussing finance with your friends: who should you listen to?" Again he scans a short article with some good tips, and links to more in-depth reading. Mason is starting to feel this website could be useful and relevant for him.

He starts to print out articles—his dial-up is expensive and he will have time on the bus and during his lunch break to read them. He prints out five. Then he ends his online session and takes the articles to work.

*Using scenarios increases the return on investment on your research*

## Sharing research with the team

Note how the example scenario describes the interaction with the website, not the website design. When designing, you will test these scenarios regularly to see if your persona can still fulfill their goals with your website. If they can, you are on the right track. Further scenarios can be developed for each important moments the personas will enter, exit or interact with your site.

The advantage of scenarios is that they offer a very efficient way to discuss and design for real users. Using personas and scenarios means that your user research isn't just sitting on a shelf gathering dust; it is being put to use. Using scenarios increases the return on investment in your research.

When doing any type of research, sharing the data and interpretations with your team is crucial. Writing a document summing up your conclusions is usually not enough. It can be more useful to have a few meetings to discuss the data, and hang some of the results on a wall in the office. Research documents often don't get read, but everyone will look at a research poster hanging in the office kitchen.

**Scenario 3**

Persona: Richard

Age: 49

Occupation: Company director

Scenario: Richard already feels in control of his finances but visits the site after noticing an advertisement in the press for this new financial site. He already banks online and manages his stocks and shares in the same way, but is interested in new products that may help him—he is considering changing his pension, so would like comparative information.

Richard reads two news articles on pensions, checks the comparative rates and benefits on the site's pension tracker, and bookmarks the site for future reference.

**Presenting research data and conclusions**

Presenting research in a meeting meant for discussion is a great way of increasing the value of the research: it keeps the team focused on the audience of the website. If you organize a meeting like this, keep it lively. Giving boring presentations is going to give research a bad name, so don't do it. Don't use numbers in your presentation (especially percentages), and don't use graphs—unless you are presenting to a client. Instead, use lots of relevant quotes from real people: print them out in a large font and hang them on the walls of the meeting room. Use pictures and tell stories to convey a feeling for your target audience.

*When presenting data use lots of relevant quotes from real people*

IMAGINE HOW YOUR DIFFERENT PERSONAS WILL REACT TO CERTAIN SCENARIOS TO ENSURE THAT YOUR SITE CATERS FOR ALL OF YOUR TARGET USERS' GOALS

*Designing a website based on audience research does not mean letting the audience decide what the website should look like or how it should work*

## Conclusion

All this research may seem a bit overwhelming, but remember that these are just design techniques that are used to prepare for the design process: a thorough understanding of the people you design for is the best preparation for a designer. Use whatever methods you feel will help you to make design decisions.

I want to stress an important point: designing a website based on audience research does not mean letting the audience decide what the website should look like or how it should work. You decide that. The audience research will let you better understand the people you design for; nothing more. Letting your audience drive design is simply bad design methodology. Focusing your design on the audience is good design methodology. You make the decisions.

Just like your favorite illustration program, the better you know these research tools, the more useful they become. Learning to use them can only make you more effective at what you do, and the more you use them, the better you'll become.

## Learning more...

The term "contextual inquiry" was coined by Meyer and Holzblatt and is described in their excellent book *Contextual Design*. It's a classic. *Don't Make me Think* by Steve Krug is the best introductory book around about ease of use and usability testing techniques. If you don't own it already, order it today. Personas and scenarios are techniques developed by Alan Cooper and described in detail in the book *The Inmates are Running the Asylum*. He has a useful website at

**www.** http://cooper.com.

**TEAMWORK**
**It is always useful to sit with your team members and discuss your ideas as you examine work on the project. Explaining your reasons for changes will build common understanding in the future.**

*Use whatever techniques you feel help you make design decisions*

# Case study: Pottery Barn Kids
# potterybarnkids.com

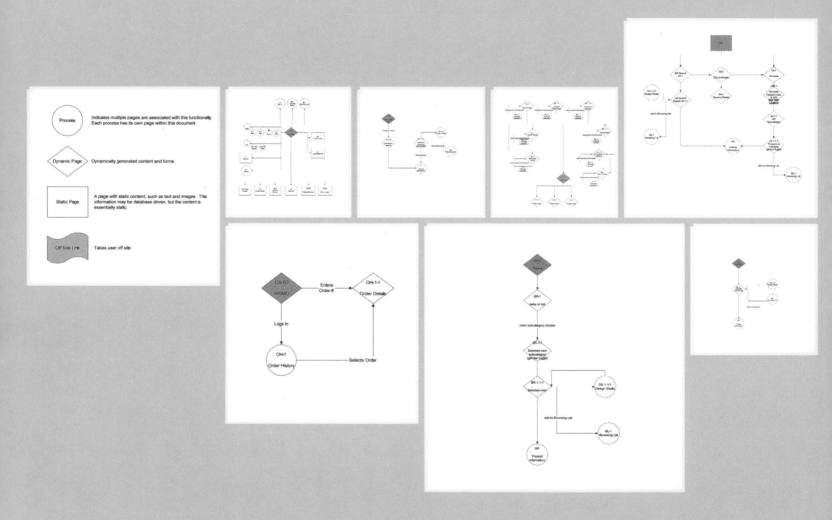

**PROCESS FLOWS**
**These flow charts are a result of an early stage in the design, when it was necessary to map proposed functionality for discussion. These show how parts of the website work. Chapter 4, page 123, explains flow charts in detail.**

**Pottery Barn Kids, a division of Pottery Barn furniture and lifestyle store, was a two-year-old catalog retailer when it decided to embark on a web presence. Addis (www.addis.com) was hired to design the site.**

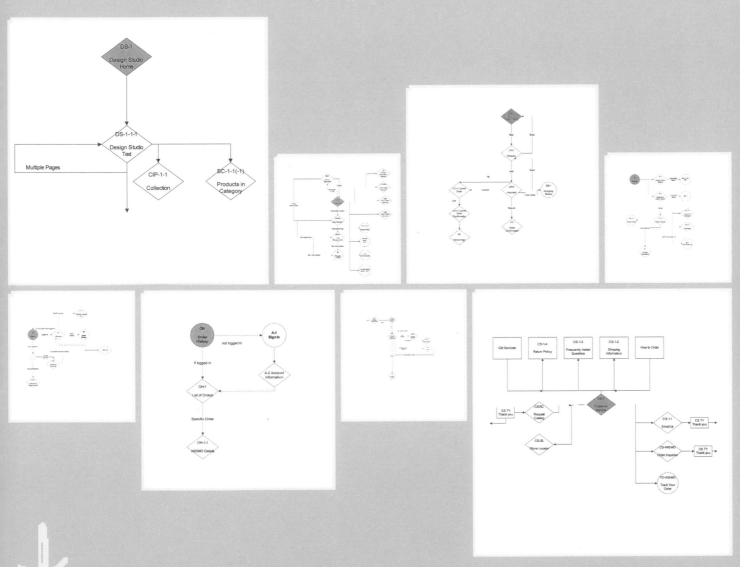

*A potential customer doesn't want to be overwhelmed with an array of furniture that isn't appropriate*

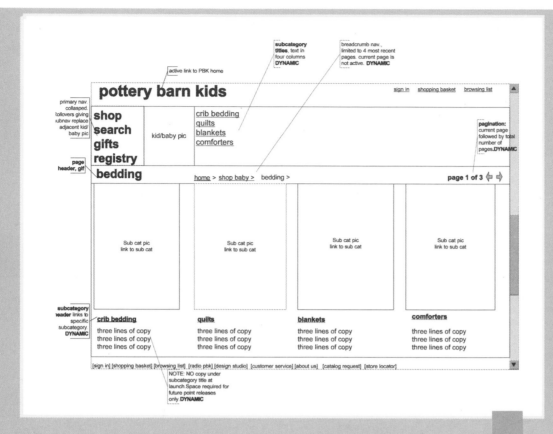

- active link to PBK home
- **subcategory titles**, text in four columns **DYNAMIC**
- breadcrumb nav., limited to 4 most recent pages. current page is not active. **DYNAMIC**

pottery barn kids

sign in    shopping basket    browsing list

- primary nav. collasped. rollovers giving subnav replace adjacent kid/ baby pic

**shop**
**search**
**gifts**
**registry**
**bedding**

kid/baby pic

crib bedding
quilts
blankets
comforters

- **pagination:** current page followed by total number of pages.**DYNAMIC**

- page header, gif

home >  shop baby >   bedding >

page 1 of 3

- subcategory header links to specific subcategory. **DYNAMIC**

Sub cat pic
link to sub cat

Sub cat pic
link to sub cat

Sub cat pic
link to sub cat

Sub cat pic
link to sub cat

**crib bedding**
three lines of copy
three lines of copy
three lines of copy

**quilts**
three lines of copy
three lines of copy
three lines of copy

**blankets**
three lines of copy
three lines of copy
three lines of copy

**comforters**
three lines of copy
three lines of copy
three lines of copy

[sign in] [shopping basket] [browsing list]    [radio pbk]  [design studio]   [customer service]  [about us]    [catalog request]   [store locator]

NOTE: NO copy under subcategory title at launch.Space required for future point releases only. **DYNAMIC**

**WIREFRAMES AND FINISHED PAGES**
Once research was complete, wireframes were created to indicate where elements should be placed on the page. These detailed content unobscured by styling. The finished pages shown alongside demonstrate how graphic design completed the process.

# pottery barn kids

shop
search
gifts
registry

baby

kids

⛵SALE

Reduced prices on great products for nurseries & kids' rooms.

baby sale

kids' sale

shop room ▪ design studio ▪ customer service ▪ about us ▪ stores ▪ email me ▪ catalog request ▪ catalog quick shop ▪ potterybarn.com

Call 24 hours a day 800.993.4923

© Pottery Barn Kids 2002. All Rights Reserved. Privacy Policy

**Business goals...**

The PBK's business goal was to project the PBK brand of tasteful, quality furniture for children of different ages. PBK wanted to position itself as a helpful resource for the busy target audience. PBK would be the reliable expert in appropriate furnishings, offering selection and guidance through articles on how to make their children's environment delightful.

**and user goals...**

Working with strategists from Prophet (www.prophet.com) and the PBK company, audience research had already revealed that while PBK wished to reach grandparents and relatives, the typical PBK customer was a mother in her mid to late 30s with a graduate degree and a significant income. It also showed that the audience first approached her child's furnishings/beddings by age, then gender. For example, babies and children have different furniture needs—cribs vs. beds, or changing tables vs. play desks. A potential customer doesn't want to be overwhelmed with an array of furniture that isn't appropriate— they want to see only the furniture suitable for their child. This was surprising for the creative team, who would have assumed without research that parents are looking for specific furniture; for example beds, tables, or rugs. Research is at its best when it surprises you.

*There was a growing need for a non-specific look— dinosaurs for everyone!*

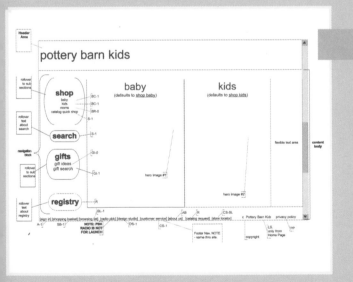

*Organizing the website around the way the audience approached the subject matter made it much more intuitive and easy to use*

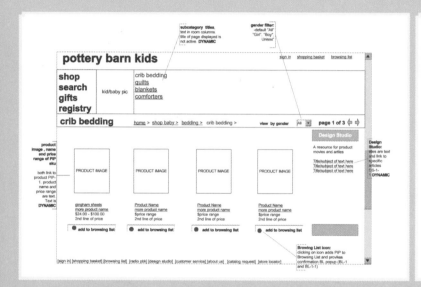

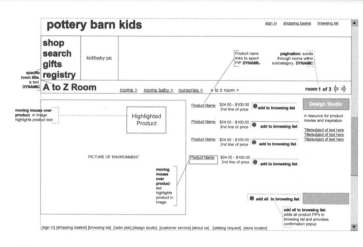

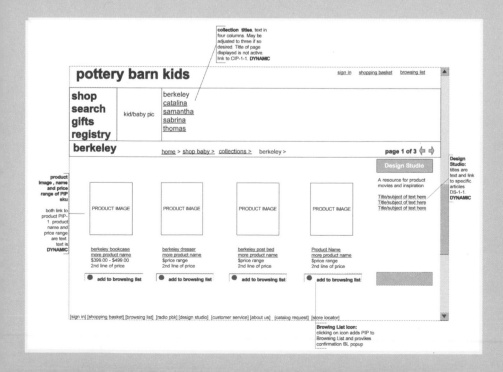

**WIREFRAMES**
**Further wireframes produced for the new website prior to the finished designs.**

### ...influence design

The fact that customers would want to select by age first had important implications for the information architecture and the design of the website. There were many internal discussions on how this would work—wouldn't customers want to see all the curtains, not just specifically baby curtains? The decision was made to present the age filter at the homepage as the initial entry into PBK products. A customer can select Baby, Kids, Rooms, Catalog Quick Shop (for those having the paper catalog on hand and a specific item in mind rather than browsing through the site) Search, and Gifts. So the initial direct access to the product catalog was by age (Baby or Kids); then particular (Furniture or Furnishings), following the audience research results.

The PBK merchants also directed the design team to create a gender filter at the product subcategory level. Again, based on their experience, the merchants saw a need to present products with a certain gender in mind. What was surprising was the certain need for a "neutral" gender. Of course, it couldn't be call "neuter," so a less offensive label was chosen. While the PBK customers liked selecting traditionally gendered looks, there was a growing need for a non-specific look—dinosaurs for everyone!

The search feature was also designed to cope with another scenario; the customer looking for products with a specific baby or child in mind, who used the PBK merchandizing experience as a helpful guide. The solution allowed for age/gender selection while maintaining a sense of whimsy and delight that was the essence of the PBK brand.

Organizing the website around the way the audience approached the subject matter made it much more intuitive and easy to use. The audience research had a determining influence on the information architecture of the website.

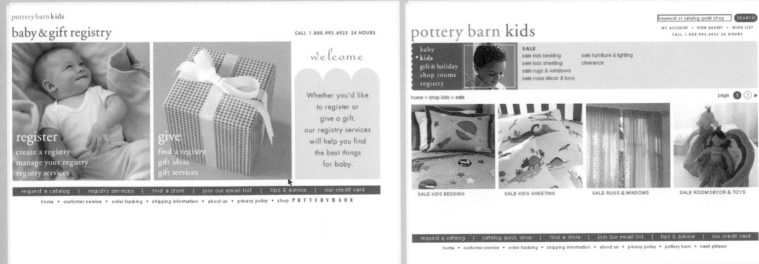

# How will you score?

Take a practice test and find out how you'd score before test day.

FREE GMAT practice test in Hoboken.

Location: The Hoboken School

Time:

Call and reserve your seat today!

**KAPLAN**

1-800-KAP-TEST

kaptest.com

Test Prep, Admissions and Guidance. For life.

PIANO

*A Professional Pian*

*Accompanist*

♪ MA from the Academy

♪ Faculty member of the
of music,

♪ 10 years experience with
adults,

♪ lessons in your home,

Please call

212–340–477

201–798–640

VALLS

FINISHES

PAINTING

EXTENSIVE
PORTFOLIO

will

ore?

*Music From Groun*

LOVE, HOPE, REMEM

# Information architecture

This chapter discusses how to create a website structure or information architecture based on the goals of the user and the business. The information architecture of the website is hard to see in action—it is mostly perceived through navigation elements.

The invisibility of information architecture means it is often ignored, but whether you know it or not, if you design a website you are creating information architecture. And you'll be better if you know what you're creating.

The basic skills needed for information architecture are an understanding of how we categorize things, and an understanding of the user. If you've read the previous chapter and implemented some of the techniques discussed there, you already have a good understanding of your user. Now it's time to think about categorization on your website.

We all categorize the world constantly. Thinking about categorization can be surprisingly hard though, because it comes so naturally to us—we have rarely had to think about it consciously before.

Defining information architecture is often skipped in favor of doing visual design or coding, the more visible aspects of web development. However, having an unsatisfactory structure in place can be very costly, both in terms of customer satisfaction and future scaling and adjusting of the website.

# Organization schemes, categories, and labels

Information architecture means organizing a website so it is easy to use and easy to find things. In this section I will introduce some concepts crucial for organizing websites: organization schemes, categories, and labels.

*An understanding of the audience drives information architecture decisions*

## Organization schemes

These are ways of organizing information. Time-based organization is one example; a news website will show the most recent news first and the news items are organized around the idea of time. Subject-based organization is another scheme; the same news website will also allow people to see news by subject: World News, Sports, Science, and so on. Task-based organization is a third popular organization scheme; our news website will probably also have a list of tasks, things you can do on the website—Search, Adjust Your Profile, Email This Page, and so on. There are many possible organization schemes; determining which ones to use on your website is the focus of the first part of this chapter.

## Categories

After determining organization schemes, you must define categories. In the subject-based organization scheme for our news website, "World News" is a category, as is "Sports." The information architect has to define the list of categories for each organization scheme, making sure all the contents fit comfortably into the choice of category; that the categories will scale as the website evolves; and that they make sense to the user.

## Labels

These are the actual words you use to define specific categories on your site. Our category World News could be called just World (CNN and BBC), or The World (LA Times) or International (NY Times). Labels must be chosen so the users of the website will easily know what they mean.

"Were you expecting a single definition? Something short and sweet? A few words that succinctly capture the essence and expanse of the field of information architecture? Keep dreaming!"
**Lou Rosenfeld and Peter Morville,**
*Information Architecture for the World Wide Web*

"Interaction design and information architecture sound like esoteric, highly technical areas, but these disciplines aren't really about technology at all. They are about understanding people, the way they work, and the way they think. By building this understanding into the structure of our product, we help ensure a successful experience for those who have to use it."
**Jesse James Garret**
*The Elements of the User Experience— User-centered Design for the Web*

"Yes, there is too much stuff on the web. Yes, it needs to be organized. But how? If you are like me, you are feeling like you're facing spring cleaning and all you can do is sit on the couch and stare at the mess."
**Christina Wodtke**
*Information Architecture— Blueprints for the Web*

| Front Page | MAIN PAGE | International |
|---|---|---|
| World | WORLD | National |
| UK | U.S. | Politics |
| UK Politics | WEATHER | Business |
| Business | BUSINESS | Technology |
| Sci/Tech | SPORTS | Science |
| Health | POLITICS | Health |
| Education | LAW | Sports |
| Entertainment | SCI-TECH | New York Region |
| Talking Point | SPACE | Education |
| In Depth | HEALTH | Weather |
| AudioVideo | ENTERTAINMENT | Obituaries |
| | TRAVEL | NYT Front Page |
| | EDUCATION | Corrections |
| | IN-DEPTH | |

PP99

"Defining information architecture is a reoccurring theme in all IA forums, and frequently leads to renaming efforts as well, from information therapist to experience designer."
**Eric Scheid, Information Architect**

WWW. NYTIMES.COM
WWW. CNN.COM
HTTP://NEWS.BBC.CO.UK/
The topic organization schemes of these three news websites show different categories (notice the BBC don't have a Sports section, and only the *New York Times* has Obituaries) and different labels for categories (World vs. International). Also note the different ordering of categories. CNN shows Weather as the third category. This might seem a bit strange for a news website, until you realize that business travellers are a core audience of CNN, and they want to know the weather at their destination. Understanding the audience drives information architecture decisions.

## News Front Page

World

UK

England

N Ireland

Scotland

Wales

Politics

Business

Entertainment

Science/Nature

Technology

Health

Education

## BBC NEWS    BBC SPORT

### Change Edition

**The World Edition** gives prominence to World news, business, and sport along with international radio and TV. All UK stories are also available in this edition. You are likely to use this edition if you live outside the UK.

< CANCEL        Continue to WORLD EDITION >

HTTP://NEWS.BBC.CO.UK/ (WORLD EDITION)
HTTP://NEWS.BBC.CO.UK/ (UK EDITION)

Sometimes your audiences are so different for different areas of the site that you need two different information architectures and hence two different versions of the site. The BBC have split their news and sports sites up into two sections: one aimed at the UK, and one at the rest of the world. Although the look of the sites is identical, the difference in audience is clearly visible in the different information architectures.

### Organization schemes

As we mentioned in the introduction of this book, there are many ways to organize the same information. Selecting useful organization schemes (there are usually more than one) is a core responsibility of an information architect. The organization schemes you choose will define the navigation on the website. Organization schemes are some of the basic building blocks of website design, yet they are often not given much attention.

Some popular ways of organizing information are:

- Task-based—websites with a lot of functionality can be organized around the things you can do on them: Buy Items, Sell Items, and Adjust your Profile on a trading website, for example.

- Audience-based—websites with clearly separate audiences such as consumers, small business, and resellers for example, who have different needs, can profit from an audience-based organization scheme

- Topical—websites with lots of content often use a topical scheme. The Yahoo homepage is organized around topics.

- Time-based—websites with time-sensitive content like news can profit from a time-based scheme.

Most websites use a mix of organization schemes. This allows users to find things in different ways. To determine which organization schemes to use, look at the tasks and goals of the users. Your understanding of the user will help you select the best organization schemes. Later in this chapter, we will describe how to work these organization schemes into a design. When working on them, jump back and forth between these steps: think of some organization schemes that would support the tasks of the users, then imagine how they would fit in the design. Then come back to refining the organization schemes.

*Most websites use a mix of organization schemes*

Task-based scheme

(logo)

Geographical scheme                    (branding)

(promotion)                            Audience-based
                                       scheme

Topical scheme

Buy Online or Call 1-800-WWW-DELL

**Choose A Country/Region**

United States

Easy as Dell.

Dell | Precision M50 Mobile Workstation

For professional workstation users who require freedom and flexibility.

**Online Shopping**

**Consumer**
Home & Home Office

**Business**
Small Business
Medium & Large Business

**Public**
State & Local Government
Federal Government
Education
Healthcare

▷ Support

**Servers & Storage**
Engineered for high
performance, maximum
uptime, serviceability, and
ease of management.

**Notebooks &
Desktops**
Harnessing the power of
emerging technology for
top performance, serious
multitasking & high
productivity.

**Networking**
Designed for high
performance, reliability and
interoperability,
PowerConnect switches
deliver unprecedented
value.

**Software &
Peripherals**
Top brands of printers,
software applications,
scanners, cameras,
handhelds and thousands
of other products.

**Services**
Dell helps provide an
outstanding end-to-end
service experience from
consulting through
deployment and support.

**www. DELL.COM**
Dell uses a classic mix of organization
schemes on their homepage: audience-
based, topical, geographical, and task-based.
Each classification scheme is clearly
distinguished in the wireframe design (right).

*There are different levels of organization to admire during a walk down a busy street*

**REAL-LIFE INFORMATION ARCHITECTURE**
There are different levels of organization to admire during a walk down a busy street. A public message board has no organization except for who posted last (they are on top). A display of fruits can be organized by price, color, size, or many other properties. And magazine stands are usually well organized: first by gender—magazines for men and women are generally separate—and then by topic. In the section for men we will find cars, movies, business, and computers; in the female section we will find fashion and lifestyle magazines.

### Categories

Once you've decided on some organization schemes, work out the categories in them. Categories are the elements of an organization scheme. For example, in a topic-based scheme for a news site, categories could be: World, Sports, Finance, and Technology. You have to make sure that all the content on the website fits somewhere into categories, and that the categories make sense to the user.

To define the categories, group your content around the way users think about the content and functionality. You don't need to use final names for your categories yet; you can call a category Everything to do With Existing Clients, and later refine that name into something like Current Customers. The category stays the same; the name can be changed.

One interesting way of coming up with categories is to use the card-sorting technique described in Chapter 2, page 60. Instead of doing the sorting yourself, you have people of the target audience do it to find out how they organize things. Write the title or content of about 50 typical pages of the website on cards, put them on a table, and get people from the target audience to sort them into categories. Let them write their own categories. Repeat this with five people and you should have a good grasp of how the people of your target audience categorize the content on your website. Pay specific attention to the words they use for the categories. Then use your own knowledge and common sense to work the results into a set of suitably named categories.

When working on categories, try to make them exclusive; if an item fits into one category in a certain scheme, it's always best if it doesn't fit in another category as well—that just confuses people. It's not always possible to make categories exclusive—sometimes you just have to place something in two categories—but it's a good thing to try for.

Categories are often organized into hierarchies. A hierarchy is a similar structure to that of a tree. For example, in a hierarchical geographic organization scheme, you could have Countries > USA > NY > New York City > Manhattan. In a topical scheme you could have Technology > Biotechnology. Hierarchies are often useful ways to organize categories, but there are other ways. Faceted classification is an advanced classification technique that works better for certain types of content. There is an example of this on pages 106–107.

Your goal is to end up with a number of organization schemes, each with a list of categories. Check if all current and future content can find a logical place in these categorization schemes. Also check if your organization makes it easy for people to find things. A good test to see if you have created good categories is this: show the category names to people, and give them a list of content items on your website. Then ask them where they would expect these items to fit.

*Two-word labels like Home & Garden are a common technique used to be more descriptive while keeping the label short*

"For a recent project, we did several rounds of usability testing, ranging from card sorting to hiring an outside company to conduct extensive usability tests nationwide. The card sorting provided great feedback in the beginning: it gave us a first-hand view of how employees used the intranet, what they wanted to see on the homepage, and which sites were frequently used. The outside company that conducted the usability tests provided an external perspective to the feedback we received."
**Heidi Gunderson, Web Consultant**

"I always get users to do a card-sorting exercise, on both large and small projects. Not only does it help me to understand what information belongs together, it is also a practical and fun way of getting users involved in the project."
**Donna Maurer, Information Architect**

**Extend categories by combining them**

Often labels for categories are clearer when you use two words to describe them: Home & Garden, Autos & Motorsports, Computer & Internet. Using two words for a label means not only that a user will understand that the category is about Home and about Garden, the user will also create a category in their heads that encompasses everything in between, and is much wider than just the two categories combined. For examples of this approach, visit:

http://epinions.com or
http://yahoo.com.

## Find Top Rated Products

### Arts & Entertainment
Books, Movies, Music...

### Autos & Motorsports
Cars, Boating, Motorcycles...

### Computers & Internet
Hardware, Software, Games...

### Electronics
DVD, Cameras, Cell Phones...

### Home & Garden
Tools, Appliances, Cooking...

### Hotels & Travel
Hotels, Destinations, Airlines...

### Kids & Family
Toys, Strollers, Car Seats...

### Personal Finance
Brokers, Banks, Credit Cards...

### Restaurants & Gourmet
Restaurants, Beers, Wines...

### Sports & Outdoors
Skis, Golf, Bikes, Parks...

### Wellness & Beauty
Nutrition, Skin Care, Fitness...

---

## BROWSE

### Featured Stores

- Apparel & Accessories
- Office Products

### Books, Music, DVD

- Books
- DVD
- Magazine Subscriptions
- Music
- Video

### Electronics & Office

- Electronics
- Audio & Video
- Camera & Photo
- Office Products

---

## Halfords Online Store

product range

- gift ideas
- winter motoring
- audio & security
- car care
- workshop & tools
- styling
- car enhancement
- bikes & toys
- cycle accessories
- child safety
- touring & travel
- load carrying

---

**WWW.** EPINIONS.COM
Epinions is a subject-based organization scheme that contains an excellent list of categories, organized in a hierarchy. Note the alphabetical presentation of the categories. Also note how many categories in the top level of the hierarchy consist of two words: Arts & Entertainment, Home & Garden, Hotels & Travel.

**WWW.** AMAZON.COM
Amazon also uses subject-based organization, based on categories and sub-categories of merchandise sold.

**WWW.** HALFORDS.COM
This retailer combines icons and subject-based categorization to represent the areas of the online store. Notice how the first category is the more inspirational Gift Ideas, for users who are not yet focused on a particular goal, followed by specific areas for those who know exactly what they are looking for.

## Labels

Labels are what we call things. A homepage could be called Home or Homepage or Welcome. Do you use About Us or Company information? These things matter; good labels make it easy for people to find what they are looking for. The information architect often spends quite a bit of time on finding the right labels for things.

The number one rule with labelling is to use the same labels as the target audience uses. Speak the language of the user. If you don't, how can you expect them to understand you? You can find out what labels they use by asking them what they call things. A typical example of bad labelling happens when a website uses the internal language of a large company that nobody outside of that company understands: Fulfillment isn't a label all users will understand, even though everyone inside the company knows exactly what it means.

When deciding on labels, focus on clarity. Be as clear as you possibly can; using the wrong word on a label can have a huge effect on the ease of use of your website. Sometimes one badly labelled button can mean a lot fewer sales—usability testing often uncovers cases like these. Look for possible confusion: could the different labels you have possibly be understood as pointing to the same thing?

Test your labels: write them down and ask members of the target audience where they would click to find certain pages on your site. If there is confusion, keep looking for better labels.

Use your labels consistently. If your shopping basket is called Shopping Basket, don't refer to it as Shopping Cart on your website. That just confuses people.

Web designers have a tendency to use short labels. They just fit better in the design. However, clear and distinctive labels are more important than short labels. Making labels longer for clarity sometimes means a trade-off with space in the design, but good labels are a big part of what helps people to find things. Try to keep them short, but don't skimp on label length at the expense of clarity.

**Don't try to decide on labels in a meeting**

Labels should be decided upon by the information architect, not by a committee. This doesn't mean you shouldn't get feedback from everyone involved; it just means that at the end of the day, you should sit down yourself and decide on the correct labels. Trying to decide on labels in a meeting just doesn't work.

**Don't use a company's internal organization scheme**

A common mistake is to use a company's internal organization scheme for the website. This will seem very logical to people within the company, but often doesn't make sense for the external users of the website, who couldn't care less how the company is organized.

**REAL-LIFE LABELLING IN AIRPORT WAYFINDING**
Using longer labels can increase clarity and reduce user confusion, as witnessed by this extended label at JFK Airport. Labelling is a core task of the information architect. By the way, if you ever need to kill some time in an airport (and who doesn't?), try examining their labelling system. There is a whole field dedicated to making it easy for people to find their way around places like airports called "wayfinding." Information architecture has much in common with wayfinding.

*Focus on clarity*

*Speak the language of the user*

*The number one rule with labelling is to use the same labels the target audience uses*

**What type of car are you looking for?**

Make (eg Ford)          Model (eg Fiesta)

No Preference ⌄          No Preference ⌄

**How much do you want to spend?**

Min £ [          ]          Max £ [          ]

**Location to search**

Enter town, county or part postcode

Within [     ] miles of [          ]

**WWW. FISH4CARS.COM**
On this British car website, the audience
determines the information architecture.
Most websites selling second-hand cars have
the same structure: you can find cars by
Make and Model, Price, and Location.

**REAL-LIFE LABELLING**
Compare this real-life labelling in a New York City subway (above) with a low entrance in New York's Hoboken district (right). Labelling decisions are made by thinking about the target audience. The phrases "Watch your step" and "Watch ya noggin" mean the same— but the New York City subway would be deservedly criticized if they used the label "Watch ya noggin". A small shop in Hoboken can get away with this—here it adds character and branding.

*A New York city subway sign is not the place to add quirky character and branding, but it gives identity to a small shop in Hoboken*

# Work the information architecture into the design

Once you have a number of organization schemes with lists of categories and easily understood labels, you have to decide how to work them into the design of the website. Organization schemes and categories will drive the navigation options on the website. They will provide the words used for links, menus, and all kinds of navigation systems.

Using multiple classification schemes on one page is completely acceptable; in fact, only a few websites don't do this. It gives users different ways to find things on the website. However, it also introduces potential for confusion. If the organization schemes are not distinguished clearly, users have to read all the category labels instead of just scanning the page in order to find the organization scheme and category they are looking for. Use design to distinguish between multiple classification systems on a page.

Separating organization schemes visually makes them easier to understand for the user. Each organization scheme should have its own visual treatment, which should be kept consistent throughout the website.

Even though you should always attempt to keep the different classification schemes visually separate, mixing classification schemes is very common in top-level navigation. This is due to the website's information architecture responding to both business and user goals.

Clients often feel strongly about a new feature, and may overestimate its importance in the whole site hierarchy. Adding a top-level section may be a wrong response to the client's desire to highlight this new part of the website to its audience.

**WWW. BARNESANDNOBLE.COM**
This online bookstore mixes the classification schemes, using the horizontal navigation for broader sections of the site and the left-hand navigation for sub-sections. Centrally positioned features also provide alternate entry points for topical items.

**"Just add a tab for this new function."**

Websites evolve, and you'll regularly have clients say something like: "Just add a top-level section for this new function." Major information architecture alert!

To deal with this, it can help to refocus on the real goals of this new function, and how it relates to the overall goals of the website. You can offer alternative ways of highlighting something new that do not involve breaking the overall structure of the website:

• A promotional section on the homepage.

• A pop-up showing off the new element of the site.

• A news item if you have a mailing list.

• Links at crucial places throughout the site.

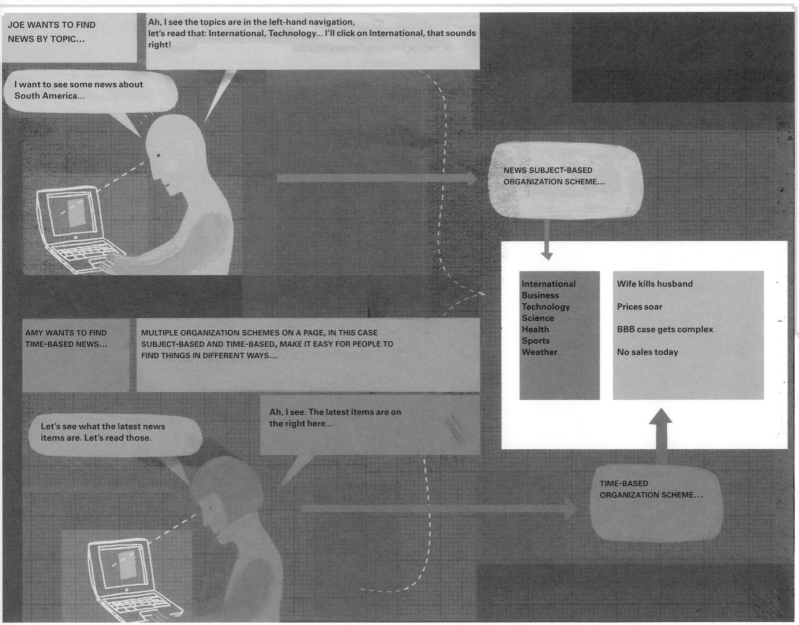

*Each organization scheme should have its own visual treatment, which should be kept consistent throughout the website*

*Use design to distinguish between multiple classification systems on a page*

*Use design to distinguish multiple classification systems on a page*

**www.** BESTCELLARS.COM
Classification systems need to be focused on the user, and few sites understand this as well as Best Wines. Their main classification of wines is not by color (red, white, or rosé), or by country or type, but by feeling and taste. From Fizzy and Fresh to Soft and Luscious, and all the way to Sweet, Best Cellars has decided that we buy our wines by taste. This is an interesting approach.

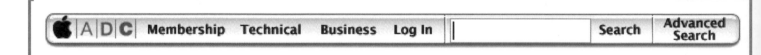

**www.** APPLE.COM
The section of the Apple website aimed at programmers uses a typical mixed classification system for their main navigation: it's organized by audience and by task. Why does the membership label come first? Because the number of members would be an important measure of success of the website, so membership needs to be highlighted. That's how business goals influence design.

*Separating organization schemes visually makes them easier to understand for the user*

FAX SERVICE • MAGAZINES
NEWS PAPERS • FILM • BATTERIES
STATIONERY • GREETING CARDS
MILK • JUICES • SOAP
DETERGENT • SHAVING SUPPLIES
SANITARY • CLEANING PRODUCTS
PAPER PRODUCTS • MEDICINES
LOTTERY • 5¢ COPY  ETC...

**APPLYING INFORMATION ARCHITECTURE TO REAL-LIFE SCENARIOS**
This is a possible organization scheme for the items found advertised in a shop window, expressed as a typical website navigation section. I organized the items in four sections: Things to Do, Household, Magazines and Newspapers, and Greeting Cards, but many other ways of organizing can be found.

**Things to do:**
Send a fax, Make a copy, Play the lottery

**Household**
Medicines, Shaving supplies, Cleaning products, Juices, Milk, Film, Batteries, Stationery, more

**Magazines & newspapers**
Bride, Wired, The New York Times, more

**Greeting cards**
Birthday, Tourism, more

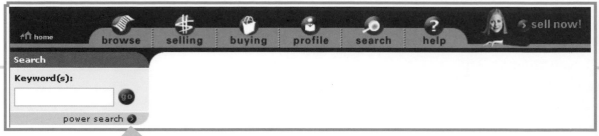

**1**

CONFUSING NAVIGATION
The top-level navigation of this website uses a confusing mix of organization schemes and labels, and the Search tab is redundant with the search positioned right under the toolbar. The Help tab is very unusual; help on websites should be context-specific—related to the task you are performing at a particular moment. Presenting Help as a tab suggests you will be presented with a help section; in other words, a manual. Manuals for websites are obviously bad news.

The Browse and Buying tabs are also confusing. This is a website where you can place classifieds, yet where do you go if you want to browse the classifieds for an item and then buy it? Browse or Buying? Could you tell the difference? Finally, the labelling is grammatically inconsistent; if you say Browse you should also say Sell and Buy. Or you should make it Browsing, Selling, and Buying. Consistency is important in labels.

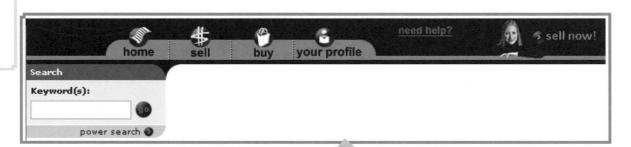

**2**

ALTERNATIVE NAVIGATION
Taking these issues into account, and noting that a redesign like this may well be missing many business or user goals taken into account by the original designers that we don't know about, alternative toolbars could look like the one above.

**3**

AUDIENCE-BASED ORGANIZATION
Business and user goals drive information architecture. If we decided there were two very different audiences for this website, we might go with an audience-based organization scheme and end up with something like the toolbar shown above.

# Enlarged Thumbnail View

Woman and child at sundown, Botswana

© #488480 Index Stock Imagery, Inc.

☰ Add To Basket

▦ Add to Lightbox

⌕ View Larger Size

Back To Previous

Image ID:
488480

Artist:
Jacob Halaska

Model Release : N
Property Release :N

Keywords:
Click on any keyword to see other images in this subject.

Adult, Baby, Child, Day, Dusk, Family, Infant, Mother, Outdoor, Parent, People, Scenic, Silhouette, Sunset, Tree, Twilight, Woman, Youth, Beauty, Africa, Horizon, Female, People 2, Botswana, Southern Africa, Backpack

*Make sure your labelling is grammatically consistent*

**WWW.** INDEXSTOCK.COM

New York-based Index Stock Imagery, Inc., is a leading source of photographs, illustrations, and digital images. Their website uses a combination of classification schemes to allow a user to refine their search: users can refine by rights, image type, color, orientation, and usage. Additionally, they use a keyword system to relate pictures about similar subjects. Making a keyword system like this successful depends on quality indexing: assigning keywords needs to be done by qualified people. Combining different classification systems can be extremely useful when users need to search through a large amount of information, or a large number of pictures as they do on this site.

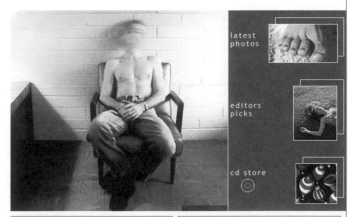

**1**  www. IBM.COM
When IBM redesigned their site, they made some important information architecture changes, based on extensive user research.

**2**  Users didn't experience Products and Consulting as two separate things they wanted to look for, so these two tabs were consolidated into Products & Services.

**3**  The News tab was removed: news is readily available from the main content area.

**4**  The About IBM tab was moved to the bottom of the page, a brave move that many companies could learn from. Users generally don't care about your company: they care about their tasks.

*When IBM redesigned their site, they made some important information architecture changes*

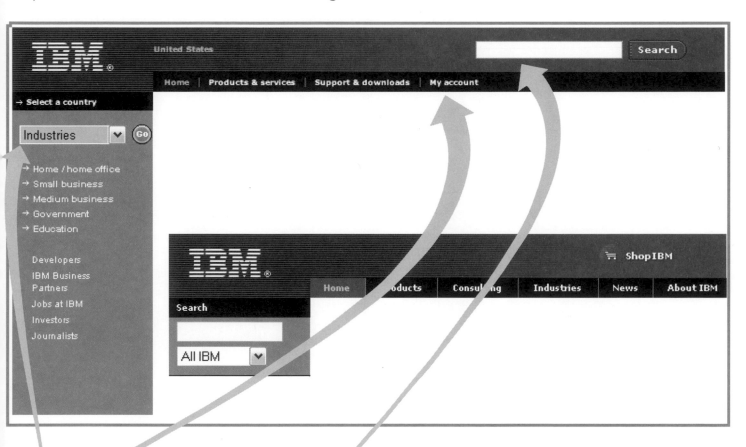

 **Industries was made into a drop-down, and a My Account tab was added, promoting the personalization features of the new website.**

**6** Trying to guess what could have influenced these decisions is a good exercise in understanding how user goals and business goals drive information architecture decisions. Note that the left-hand navigation uses an audience-based organization scheme. This wasn't changed in the redesign, proof that it works well for IBM. Also note the simplified search function.

*A faceted classification scheme simply means that you allow the user to combine multiple organization schemes instead of forcing them down one overarching hierarchy*

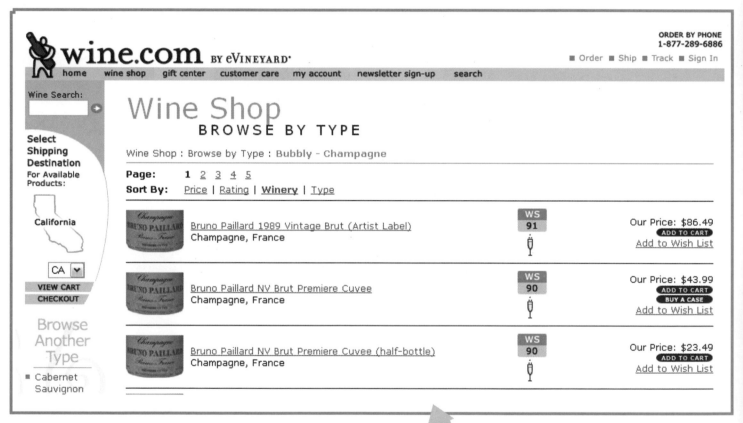

**WWW. WINE.COM**

Sometimes simple hierarchical classification just doesn't cut it. Consider wine. Do you want to organize it by region, by price, or by color? Different people will find different organization schemes useful. I may want to buy my wine by price and color, whereas you might be more interested in the country of origin.

Faceted classification comes to the rescue. A faceted classification scheme simply means that you allow the user to combine multiple organization schemes instead of forcing them down one overarching hierarchy. Each hierarchy describes a certain facet, or attribute of the product.

# wine finder

- by Type
- by Region
- by Winery

---

# Wine Shop
## BROWSE BY TYPE

Wine Shop : Browse by Type

**Are you a red wine kind of guy or gal? Or do you lean toward the bubbly? Go ahead and click on whatever category suits your fancy.**

Red Wines
White Wines
Bubbly
Pink Wines
Kosher Wines
Dessert/Fortified Wines

---

# Wine Shop
## BROWSE BY TYPE

Wine Shop : Browse by Type : Bubbly

**Now, select the varietal you'd like to browse:**

Champagne
Sparkling

Or see all of our Bubbly

---

# Wine Shop
## BROWSE BY TYPE

Wine Shop : Browse by Type : Bubbly - Champagne

**Page:**    1   2   3   4   5
**Sort By:**   Price | Rating | **Winery** | Type

Bruno Paillard 1989 Vintage Brut (Artist Label)
Champagne, France

Bruno Paillard NV Brut Premiere Cuvee
Champagne, France

---

## 2

Faceted classification systems are great for stuff that may be categorized differently by different people. Wine.com uses numerous facets and interface widgets. One on the homepage lets the user select how they want to search for wine—by type, region, and/or winery. Within each facet users can then further narrow down their options, using more facets—like price and rating—to make their selections.

www. BLUEMOUNTAIN.COM

Blue Mountain uses a mix of multiple
categorization schemes on their homepage.
The above image is a collage of the
classification schemes used by Blue Mountain.

*Multiple categorization schemes provide a huge variety of ways
for your potential customer to learn about your products*

**Blue Mountain**™     eCARDS | GIFT CENTER | SCREEN SAVERS | MUSIC GREETINGS | NEW eCARDS

celebrate Independence Day!

**FLASH!**     **FLASH!**     **FLASH!**
**Funky Fourth**  **Extravaganza**  **Fabulous 4th!**
more »        more »         more »

**top picks**
- **Summer**              • **Wedding**
- **Gifts for Anyone**    • **Anniversary**

« Top Picks »
« Top Picks »
Armed Forces
Aunt & Uncle
Best Friends
Canada
Cats
China
Dogs
Dog Breeds …

**favorites**

« Select a Category »
« Select a Category »
Anniversary
Astrology
Birthday - Belated
Birthday - Funny
Birthday - Interactive
Birthday - Romantic
Birthday - Sports
Boy Scouts
Brothers
Calendar
CardMaker
Catholic
Chinese Zodiac
Congratulations
Cumpleaños
Fall
Fathers
Games
Get Well
Girl Scouts
Good Luck
Graduation
Hindu
Housewarming
Husband
Invitations
Islamic
Jewish
Kids Awards

**channels**

**Just Because**
Say Hi | more »

**Friendship**
Interactive | more »

**Stay in Touch**
Please Write | more »

**Love**
I Love You | more »

**Astrology**
Horoscopes | more »

**Encourage/Support**
Sympathy | more »

**Extended Family**
Grandchildren | more »

**Career**
Armed Forces | more »

**Living**
Golden Years | more »

**Music Greetings**
Sheryl Crow | more »

**National & Regional**

**Pets & Nature**

**Awareness & Activism**

**Birthday**
For Everyone | Interactive | Funny
Family | Belated | Poetry | Romantic
Horoscopes | Over the Hill | **more »**

**Fun & Games**
CardMakers | Games | I-Ching
Flash Picks | Chinese Zodiac
Mousetrails | **more »**

**Kids**
For Every Kid | Proud Parent
Awards | Girl Scouts | Boy Scouts
Crafts | Reading | **more »**

**Family**
Mothers | Fathers | Sisters
Daughters & Sons | Brothers
Husbands & Wives | **more »**

**Religion**
Catholic | Bible Verse | Protestant
Jewish | Hindu | Islamic | Buddhist
Sikh | Bahá'i | **more »**

**Seasons**
Spring | Summer | Fall | Winter

**Expressions**
Thank You | Get Well | Good Luck
You're Welcome | Quotes & Quips
Congratulations | **more »**

**Celebrations & Events**
Anniversary | Graduation | Wedding
New Baby | Pregnancy | Invitations
Housewarming | **more »**

**Arts & Letters**
Susan Polis Schutz | Fine Art
Shakespeare Sonnets | Dance
Classical Poetry | **more »**

**Teens**
Friends | Say Hi | Let's Hang Out
Crush | Sorry | Good Luck
Congrats | **more »**

**Holidays**
Independence Day | Summer
Christmas in July | Calendar
**more »**

Card Pick Up Window

**2**

The image above shows the category boxes
on the homepage, rearranged to show only
organization schemes (everything not
related to categories was removed from this
homepage screengrab). Can you spot the
following categorization schemes: by
popularity, by occasion, by emotion, by
current holiday, by recipient, and by card
type. Can you find ways to improve the
design of this page given what we have
discussed in this chapter?

# Sitemaps

The classic deliverable of the information architect, sitemaps are used for communication within the team. I am talking about sitemaps for developers here, not the sitemaps for users that go on the website.

There are many ways of doing sitemaps, but before we give some examples, here are three things you should know when creating a sitemap:

- The map depends on its use—how you design your sitemap depends on the type of project and the structure of your team.

- Sitemaps are for communication, not for decorating the office.

- Make sitemaps easy to change—changes are inevitable and shouldn't take long to implement.

Sitemaps are used in discussions about the website, and by the development team when building the website. There is a tendency to make sitemaps look really good and treat them as beautiful objects to be admired by clients and team members alike. If it means the maps become less flexible, this is bad. Sitemaps are for discussion and teamwork. They provide a means for a group of people to talk about a website by having a visual representation of it. Sitemaps should follow the flow of ideas, not the other way around, so they need to be easy to change.

*Sitemaps should follow the flow of ideas, not the other way around, so they need to be easy to change*

**"Can you make a quick sitemap for this?"**

Sometimes an ill-informed project manager will get the impression that making a sitemap is just a matter of illustrating something that doesn't need much thought. Usually they are wrong. Make it clear to them that the job of the information architect isn't so much illustrating the website's structure in a sitemap, it's finding the right structure. Making a sitemap is easy; finding the right structure isn't.

## The classic sitemap

The classic sitemap shows all the pages on a website. When you have many pages of the same type (say, news articles), only one is usually shown. The map is useful for the client, to discuss the website; for the visual designers, to design all the different types of pages; and for the programmers, as a reference to what pages need to be programmed.

A sitemap indicates the hierarchy between pages by connecting them with arrows and grouping them visually. You shouldn't try to indicate every link between every page on the website. Instead, just draw connections between pages that are connected hierarchically.

A sitemap usually shows the depth of the website: how many clicks it takes to get to the last page. A deep hierarchy has the advantage of having limited options on the homepage, thus keeping things simple. A shallow hierarchy has the advantage of showing lots of options on the homepage, thus making it easier to find what you want. You'll notice both approaches try to make it easier to find things—the discussion on what approach works best is still raging in information architecture circles.

Each page on the sitemap should have at least a unique identifier: a number or a page name, or both, that identifies the page. You can then add a lot of other information to the sitemap, depending on how it will be used. Some useful things to indicate on a sitemap are:

- Which pages need special attention from the programmers.

- Access levels: which pages can be accessed only by subscribers to the website—those people who are logged in.

- Non-HTML pages like Flash, PDF.

- What type of navigation will appear on the page.

- Type of page: articles, overview pages, forms…

Most people use diagramming software to make sitemaps. It keeps connections between pages when you drag them around, so you can rearrange the sitemap quickly. Popular diagramming software packages are Microsoft Visio, ConceptDraw, and Inspiration. Links to these and other packages can be found on the website ⊟. However, you can create sitemaps in any drawing software, or even in programs like PowerPoint.

*Sitemaps are for communication, not for decorating the office*

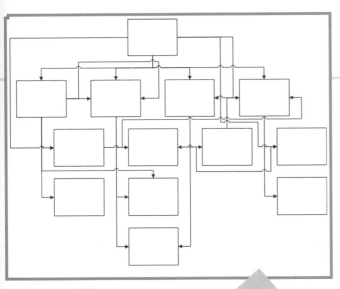

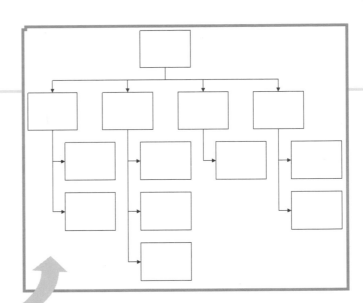

**SITEMAPS AND LINKS**
A sitemap showing all the links between pages (above) is far more confusing than a sitemap that only shows hierarchical connections (above right).

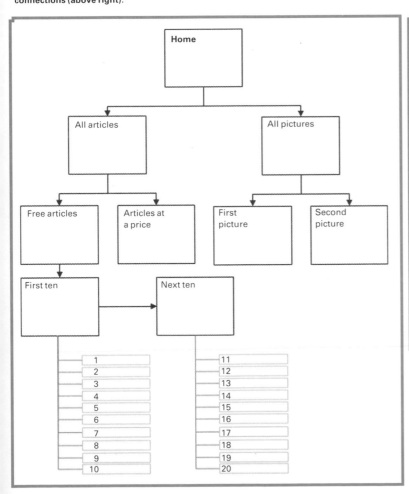

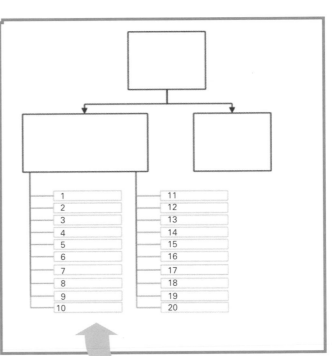

**DEEP AND SHALLOW HIERARCHIES**
The sitemap of a deep hierarchy (left) shows that it will take five clicks to reach article no.12. The sitemap above shows a shallow hierarchy. Here it only takes two clicks to reach no.12.

*Making a sitemap is easy. Finding the right structure isn't*

*There are many ways of doing sitemaps*

**PRICE WATCH®**    [Search Site]    About  **Specials**    **Software**    **Not Exactly New**    **Electronics**    **Home**

New Computer Components

| Systems | CPU | Memory | Storage | Multimedia | Input |
|---|---|---|---|---|---|
| PC - Windows | Motherboards | System | Hard Drives | Multimedia | Keyboards |
| PC - Apple | Motherboard Combos | Notebook | CDRom Drives | Video Cards | Mice |
| PC - Kits | Motherboard Accessories | Printer | CD Recorders | Video Capture | Scanners |
| Pen Tablets | CPU | Flash Card | DVD Drives | Sound Cards | WebCams |
| Notebooks | CPU - Mobile | Video | DVD Accessories | Music Hardware | Digitizers/Tablets |
| Hand Held | Cases | | Tape Drives | | Bar Code |
| Hand Held Accessories | Case/CPU Accessories | **I/O** | Removable | | Magnetic Card |
| Servers | Fans | Controller Cards | Floppy Drives | **Other** | |
| Point Of Sale Equipment | Case Power Supply | Serial Cards | Magneto Optical | MP3 Players | |
| | | | Media | MP3 Accessories | |
| **For Notebooks** | **Output** | **Networking** | Media Other | Desk Accessories | |
| Notebook Battery | Monitors | Modems | | Backup Supplies | |
| Notebook Drives | Printers | Network Cards | | Cables | |
| Notebook Modems | Plotters | Network Attached Storage | | Game Hardware | |
| Notebook Accessories | Printer Accessories | Networking Other | | Paper Products | |
| | Presentation | | | | |

System Memory Links    [Search Category]    Quotes @15:28 - 9/17    See Brands

| | | | |
|---|---|---|---|
| $1704 - 4GB | $35  - PC2400 DDR 128MB | $24  - PC133 256MB | $8   - EDO 64MB 60ns |
| $255  - 2GB | $311 - PC2100 DDR 1024MB | $14  - PC133 128MB | $6   - EDO 32MB 60ns |
| $123  - 1GB | $99  - PC2100 DDR 512MB | $10  - PC133 64MB | $216 - RDRAM 1066MHz 512MB |
| $166 - PC3500 DDR 512MB | $45  - PC2100 DDR 256MB | $123 - PC100 1GB | $108 ▼ RDRAM 1066MHz 256MB |
| $76  - PC3500 DDR 256MB | $24  - PC2100 DDR 128MB | $32  - PC100 512MB | $61  - RDRAM 1066MHz 128MB |
| $150 - PC3200 DDR 512MB | $105 - PC1600 DDR 512MB | $24  - PC100 256MB | $158 - RDRAM 512MB |
| $67  - PC3200 DDR 256MB | $49  - PC1600 DDR 256MB | $14  - PC100 128MB | $81  - RDRAM 256MB |
| $126 - PC3000 DDR 512MB | $26  - PC1600 DDR 128MB | $10  - PC100 64MB | $46  - RDRAM 128MB |
| $66  - PC3000 DDR 256MB | $70  - PC150 512MB | $9   - PC100 32MB | $8   - RIMM |
| $118 - PC2700 DDR 512MB | $36  - PC150 256MB | $27  - FPM 128MB 60ns | $7   - Cache |
| $56  - PC2700 DDR 256MB | $22  - PC150 128MB | $12  - FPM 64MB 60ns | $61  - Apple G4 PC133 512MB |
| $118 - PC2400 DDR 512MB | $145 - PC133 1GB | $37  - EDO 256MB 50ns | $34  - Apple G4 PC133 256MB |
| $56  - PC2400 DDR 256MB | $32  - PC133 512MB | $21  - EDO 128MB 60ns | |

"Sitemaps are a useful tracking system when new pages are being added to an existing site. We once used Visio to create an interactive sitemap, linking each of the boxes to its corresponding page. Some of the pages were new and linked to a schematic; others were existing pages linked to the site. Seeing the relationship between the new and existing pages helped the client step back from the project and see the new pages in context."
**Liz Danzico, Information Architect**

**www.** PRICEWATCH.COM
**Pricewatch uses a shallow hierarchy: almost all options can be seen directly on the homepage. It doesn't take many clicks to get where you want to go, but you have to take the time to read all the options on the homepage.**

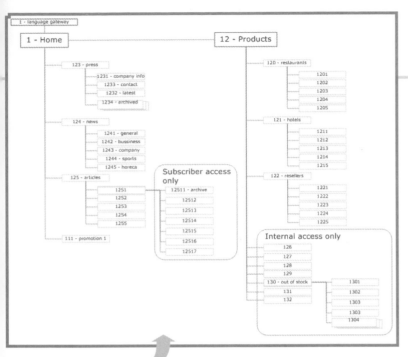

**UNIQUE IDENTIFIERS**
Each page of a sitemap should carry some distinguishing feature, for ease of identification. A numbered system is often most appropriate.

## A visual vocabulary
Creating a visual vocabulary for your sitemaps will allow you to reuse elements easily, and it will make it easier for everyone to understand the map. Creating a vocabulary like this can be quite a bit of work, but information architect Jesse James Garrett has done much of the hard work for you, and created a useful visual vocabulary for sitemaps that is becoming a standard for information architects.

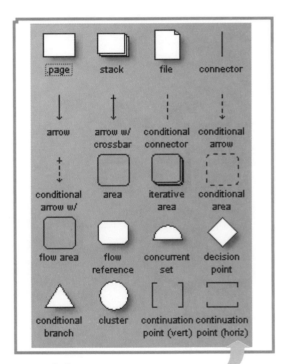

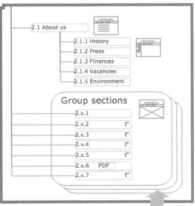

**PART OF A CLASSIC SITEMAP**
This example shows a part of a sitemap that indicates an identification number for each page, a short page title, and an indication of which template is to be used. (Note too how the number of numbers within each page also indicates the amount of clicks from the homepage.) Further information includes the file type (PDF) and check-boxes for the developers indicating where functionality must be tested. When using sitemaps as a development tool for the first time in your team, talk to everybody who will use them and ask them what information they would like on them.

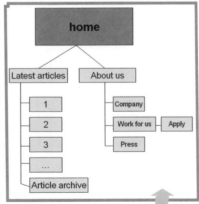

**POWERPOINT**
Creating sitemaps doesn't have to require specialist software: PowerPoint presentation software is more than adequate to illustrate simple sitemaps.

**WWW.** JJG.NET/IA/VISVOCAB
Jesse James Garrett's visual vocabulary is a useful, standardized set of shapes for making sitemaps. These can be downloaded for free (and for use with different programs).

### The 2.5D or isometric sitemap

Making a sitemap in two and a half dimensions provides interesting possibilities for showing more information on the map. It is especially useful when you want to show access levels and click depth. They are called 2.5D or isometric sitemaps because you don't use a true three-dimensional perspective whereby pages become smaller as their distance increases. An additional advantage is that they look gorgeous and are great for client presentations. There is a Visio stencil available on this book's website ⊟ for making 2.5D maps.

When building a complex map like the one below, keep in mind our rule for creating sitemaps: they should be easy to change. Whatever program you use to make the map, spend some time learning about options like layers, stencils, or backgrounds that can help you keep the map flexible.

### The automated sitemap

When mapping out an existing website for analysis, an automated tool can save you lots of time. There still doesn't exist a perfect tool for this, so you will have to do some experimentation. Many website development tools like Dreamweaver and FrontPage come with sitemapping tools, but you will still have to visit the website yourself to interpret which pages are on which level, and how they connect. A perfect tool for this still doesn't exist, so this book's website provides a variety of sitemaps ⊟.

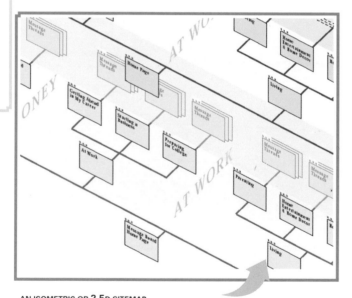

**AN ISOMETRIC OR 2.5D SITEMAP**
Isometric sitemaps can be used to illustrate access levels and they look fantastic. The complete map that this example was taken from is on page 115.

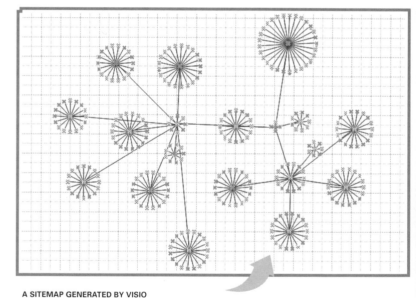

**A SITEMAP GENERATED BY VISIO**
Many web-development tools can generate sitemaps of existing websites automatically. They almost always need more work, however.

### The high-level sitemap

A high-level sitemap doesn't show all the pages on the website, but it does show the general structure. They are useful in the initial stages of the project. Things that a high-level sitemap can indicate include:

• Different sections of the website.

• Different access levels.

• Different types of functionality.

• Users of the website, and how they will interact with it.

### The content table

A content table is a list of pages with a number of properties for each page. It serves many of the same goals as a sitemap, but presents the results as a table, not as a visual map. The advantage of a content inventory table is that it is easier to add more information for each page—by just adding a column to the table—and it scales better; you can add thousands of pages without problems. The disadvantage is that you lose the visual hierarchy of a sitemap that allows you to discuss a website. A content inventory table is often used for large websites after a sitemap containing the main sections has been constructed. Another use is to build one for an existing website to clarify content.

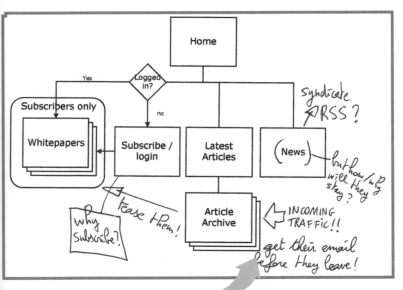

**A TYPICALLY ANNOTATED HIGH-LEVEL SITEMAP**
Providing a high-level sitemap helps discussions about the structure of the website. Notice how the map doesn't show all the pages—at this stage they would only serve to distract. Instead, it shows the sections that matter for the discussion.

**A CONTENT INVENTORY TABLE**
This is an alternative way to present the pages on a website. It is useful when needing to make constant adjustments to content, but does not show the hierarchies clearly. These tables are often used in conjunction with other forms of sitemaps.

| 1 | Link ID | Link name | Link | Document type | Owner | Keywords | ROT | Notes |
|---|---------|-----------|------|---------------|-------|----------|-----|-------|
| 2 | 1 | Homepage | http://mydomai | homepage | | | | |
| 3 | 1.1 | About us | http://mydomai | text | PR | | | |
| 4 | 1.2 | Contact us | http://mydomai | text | PR | | | |
| 5 | 1.3 | Jobs | http://mydomai | text | Human Resources | | | |
| 6 | 2 | Toys | http://mydomai | nav | Sales | | | |
| 7 | 2.1 | Small kids | http://mydomai | nav | Sales | | | |
| 8 | 2.1.1 | toys for babies | http://mydomai | product | Inventory | | | |

## Conclusion

Organization schemes, categories, and labels are all design decisions. These choices will have a great impact on the visual design of the website, and how easy it is to use. The design of this information architecture is based on an understanding of the user and business goals. In the next chapter, we'll see how to design task flows for websites that have a lot of functionality.

*Organization schemes, categories, and labels are all design decisions*

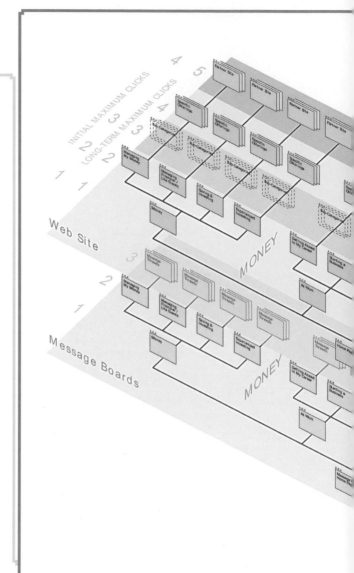

**WWW.** CLIENT.COM
**This isometric sitemap employs color, dimensionality, and standard visual vocabulary to great effect. The result is impressive and useful for presentations as well as being a key discussion tool.**

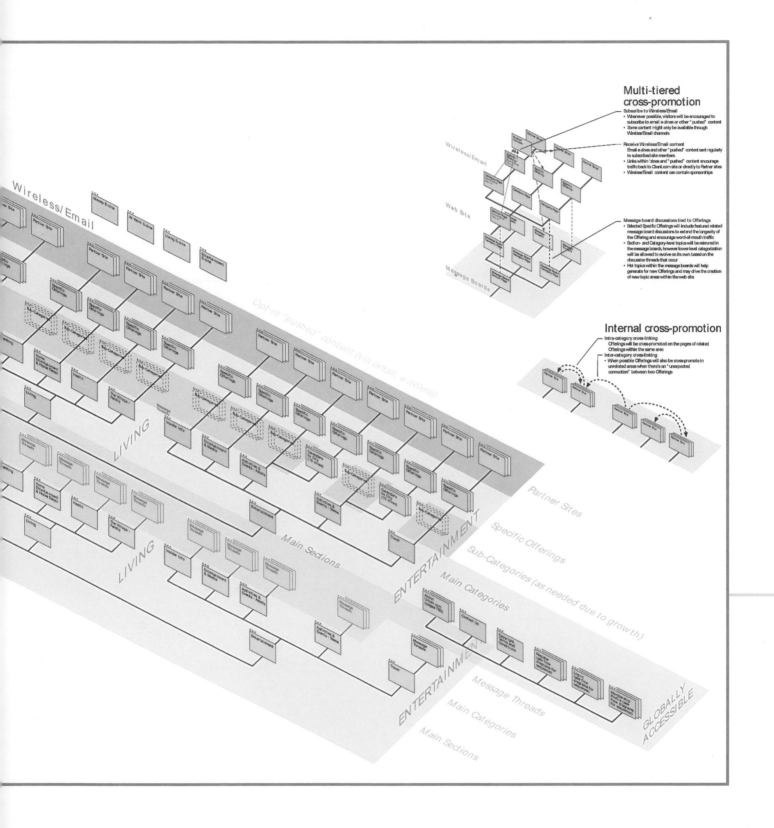

### Multi-tiered cross-promotion

**Subscribe to Wireless/Email**
- Whenever possible, visitors will be encouraged to subscribe to email e-zines or other "pushed" content
- Some content might only be available through Wireless/Email channels

**Receive Wireless/Email content**
Email e-zines and other "pushed" content sent regularly to subscribed site members
- Links within "zines and "pushed" content encourage traffic back to Client.com site or directly to Partner sites
- Wireless/Email content can contain sponsorships

**Message board discussions tied to Offerings**
- Selected Specific Offerings will include featured related message board discussions to extend the longevity of the Offering and encourage word-of-mouth traffic
- Section- and Category-level topics will be mirrored in the message board, however lower-level categorization will be allowed to evolve on its own based on the discussion threads that occur
- Hot topics within the message boards will help generate for new Offerings and may drive the creation of new topic areas within the web site

### Internal cross-promotion

**Intra-category cross-linking**
Offerings will be cross-promoted on the pages of related Offerings within the same area
**Inter-category cross-linking**
- When possible Offerings will also be cross-promote in unrelated areas when there's an "unexpected connection" between two Offerings

# Case study: Semiconductor Research Corporation (SRC) Collaborative Extranet

**www. src.org**

**THE ORIGINAL EXTRANET**
The original extranet made it hard for people to find out about research being conducted outside of their own specialized group.

*People knew what their peers were doing, but not what other groups in the organization were up to*

The Semiconductor Research Corporation (SRC) was struggling with an ever-expanding community that needed better tools for sharing research. SRC facilitates relationships between member technology companies such as Intel, IBM, and Hewlett-Packard, and engineering research programs at universities.

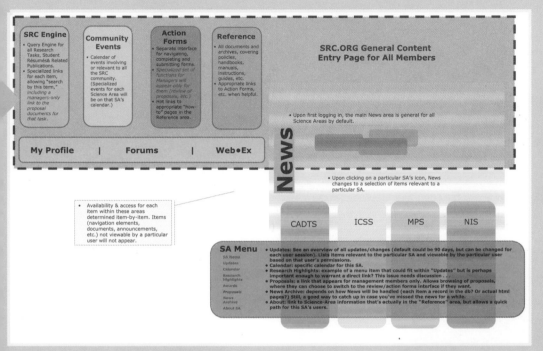

**MODELS BASED ON USER RESEARCH**
After conducting audience research using observation, interviews, and questionnaires, the design team discussed what they had learned and recorded their insights in easily referenced visual models like the three examples shown here.

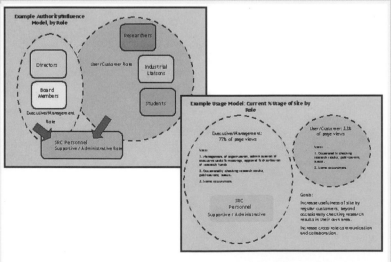

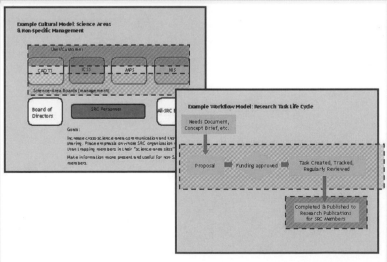

*The resulting website is not only easy to use, but also addresses the real problems of the company and the people using it*

### First find out what the problems are

Symetri (www.symetri.com) was hired as the design vendor for this project. Andrew Hinton was the lead information architect. The first thing Symetri did was audience research. They used observation, interviews, and questionnaires to truly understand the problems the target users were facing. They discovered that the growing organization was suffering from silo-proliferation: people knew what their peers were doing, but not what other groups in the organization were up to. SRC's website was their single best hope for bringing people out of their shells and into a common environment, while still providing "pockets" for specialized interests.

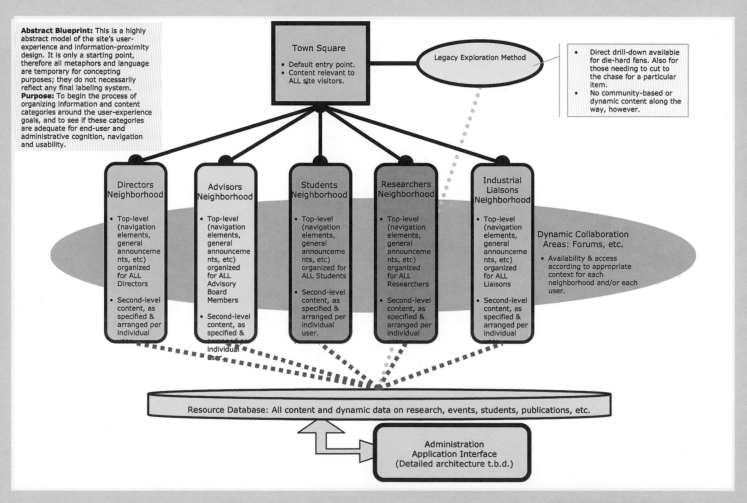

**Abstract Blueprint:** This is a highly abstract model of the site's user-experience and information-proximity design. It is only a starting point, therefore all metaphors and language are temporary for concepting purposes; they do not necessarily reflect any final labeling system.
**Purpose:** To begin the process of organizing information and content categories around the user-experience goals, and to see if these categories are adequate for end-user and administrative cognition, navigation and usability.

Town Square
• Default entry point.
• Content relevant to ALL site visitors.

Legacy Exploration Method

• Direct drill-down available for die-hard fans. Also for those needing to cut to the chase for a particular item.
• No community-based or dynamic content along the way, however.

Directors Neighborhood
• Top-level (navigation elements, general announcements, etc) organized for ALL Directors
• Second-level content, as specified & arranged per individual

Advisors Neighborhood
• Top-level (navigation elements, general announcements, etc) organized for ALL Advisory Board Members
• Second-level content, as specified & arranged per individual user.

Students Neighborhood
• Top-level (navigation elements, general announcements, etc) organized for ALL Students
• Second-level content, as specified & arranged per individual user.

Researchers Neighborhood
• Top-level (navigation elements, general announcements, etc) organized for ALL Researchers
• Second-level content, as specified & arranged per individual

Industrial Liaisons Neighborhood
• Top-level (navigation elements, general announcements, etc) organized for ALL Liaisons
• Second-level content, as specified & arranged per individual

Dynamic Collaboration Areas: Forums, etc.
• Availability & access according to appropriate context for each neighborhood and/or each user.

Resource Database: All content and dynamic data on research, events, students, publications, etc.

Administration Application Interface (Detailed architecture t.b.d.)

**EARLY ILLUSTRATION OF HIGH-LEVEL ARCHITECTURE**
After finishing the research phase, the team designed the revised website's high-level architecture. This aimed to allow people to break out of their silos, while still providing specialized areas. This diagram is an illustration of that architecture. Diagrams like these help the understanding and discussion of the proposed solution in client meetings.

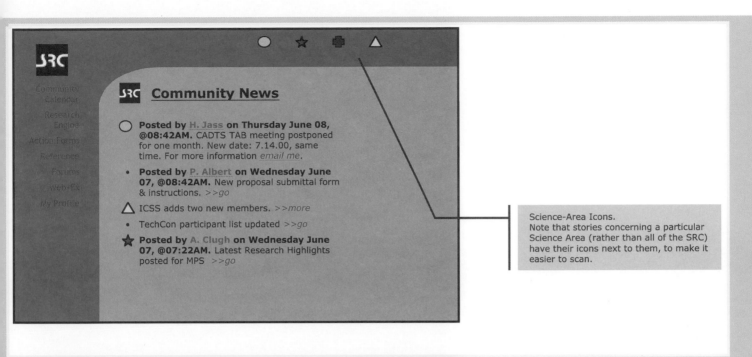

Science-Area Icons.
Note that stories concerning a particular Science Area (rather than all of the SRC) have their icons next to them, to make it easier to scan.

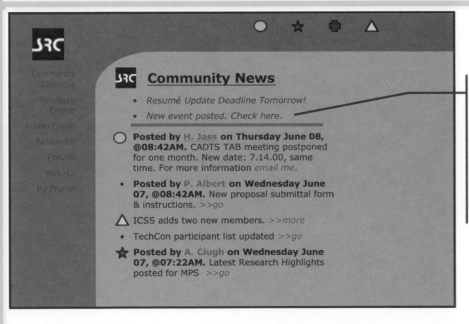

Special reminder, to-do, and other special announcement area, determined per user, based on whatever groups they are part of. Can include hotlinks to items.
Not necessarily science-area dependent.

NOTE: If the individual is in both a SA TAB and an all-SRC board, this will include both sets of announcements.

NOTE: This can be used for anybody, even if they are not "management" -- such as Students who need to update their resumes.

**WIREFRAMES AND PAPER PROTOTYPES**
The information architecture was then worked out in further detail. In the next step, wireframes and paper prototyping techniques were used to develop the user interface, which was then tested on members of the target audience.

**...Then address those problems with information architecture**
The solution for this problem was an architecture that allowed for very different individuals and sub-groups to share news with one another, organize events and documentation, and access a common "research engine" of consolidated research results. Branching off from the common "town square" are sub-sites that, while never really leaving the SRC space, provide the necessary areas for smaller neighborhoods.

SRC counts their new site as a great success; the users enjoy being able to communicate important news with the whole organization, while having an efficient means to collaborate easily with those in their own spheres of responsibility. The information architect took the problems of the target audience as a starting point. The resulting website is not only easy to use, but also addresses the real problems of the company and the people using it.

**USER INTERFACE DESIGNS**
After multiple iterations, the designs were refined into final versions ready for production.

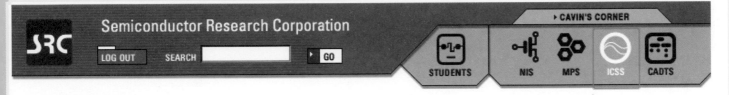

**Semiconductor Research Corporation**

▸ CAVIN'S CORNER

LOG OUT    SEARCH [        ] ▸ GO

STUDENTS    NIS    MPS    ICSS    CADTS

ABOUT
SRC CALENDAR
RESEARCH ENGINE
ACTION FORMS
REFERENCE
FORUMS @ the HUB
MY PROFILE
LINKS

TARGETED FOR

BOARD OF DIRECTORS
EXECUTIVE TAB
VALUE CHAIN TAB
STUDENT RELATIONS TAB
UNIVERSITY RESEARCHERS
SCIENCE AREA BOARDS
INDUSTRIAL LIAISONS
UAC
RECRUITERS

## ▾ SRC news

NY Governor Pataki Announces High Tech Award to Rensselaer Polytechnic Institute More

Newly Issued SRC Patent: US Patent 6,346,446 to Andrew Ritenour of the Massachusetts Institute of Technology for Methods of Forming Features of Integrated Circuits Using Modified Buried Layers More

Newly Issued SRC Patent: US Patent 6,300,649 to Chenming Hu, Mansun John Chan, Hsing-Jen Wann and Ping Keung Ko for Silicon-on-Insulator Transistors Having Improved Current Characteristics and Reduced Electrostatic Discharge Susceptibility More

Newly Issued SRC Patent: US Patent 6,352,942 to Hsin-Chiao Luan and Lionel Kimerling of Massachusetts Institute of Technology for Oxidation of silicon on germanium More

DEADLINE APRIL 17, 2002: Call for Nominations for Aristotle Award, Technical Excellence Award, and Mahboob Khan Outstanding Mentor Awards More

An online version of the 2001 SRC corporate annual report is now available. More
▯.pdf

MPS solicits new work in important FEP area: White Papers due April 19, 2002 More

2001 Aristotle Awards Presented to Professor Rob Rutenbar, Carnegie Mellon University, and to Professor Gerold Neudeck, Purdue University. More

# Designing functionality

4

You design websites, not web pages, and this distinction is most important when dealing with complex functionality. When using such websites, the user spends much time moving back and forth between multiple pages. These pages need to hang together in a coherent way, allowing different people to achieve different goals.

This chapter describes the steps in designing functionality:
1. Identifying tasks
2. Task analysis to break down tasks into small parts
3. Turning task analysis into page design
4. Documenting functionality

Even though this chapter comes after that of information architecture, designing functionality and information architecture are usually done concurrently.

## Identifying tasks

The first step in designing functionality is to examine the things people will do on the website—their tasks.

A task can be anything that supports a user goal: ordering a book, finding information, subscribing to a newsletter. Once you have a list of tasks, you can design a website that supports them in the best possible way.

The tasks your website should support are found by doing user research as described in Chapter 2. The research results in a list of goals and tasks. Tasks can be obvious ones, like Ordering a Book, but might also be Finding the Right Book, or Emailing a Friend About a Book, or Finding Related Books. Supporting non-obvious tasks is what sets great websites apart from mediocre ones.

Tasks are ordered by importance. On a website selling books, it will be more important to support the task of Finding the Right Book than the task of finding Company Information. This ordering of tasks will be reflected in the design of the website. Tasks are often different for each audience type, for example, Resellers will have different tasks on your site from Consumers.

*You design websites, not web pages*

## Analyzing tasks

Task analysis is a technique that breaks down tasks into small parts—sub-tasks. Task analysis doesn't talk about interface details, it just says what steps the user needs to take to complete a task. It is useful because it enables you to really understand all the steps a user has to take when completing different tasks—which helps a lot when designing functionality.

A task analysis is based on user research. The goal of task analysis is to find out exactly what steps the user has to take to complete a certain task. To do that, you break down the task into small steps.

Remember the financial website we used as an example in Chapter 2? Mason ("Where can I find trustworthy advice?") was looking for better ways to invest his savings. To use the site successfully, Mason will have to complete a number of tasks, the first crucial one being signing up. Task analysis can help us to better understand complex tasks like this. Let's see if we can break it down into some sub-tasks, and maybe add in some of Mason's goals:

**Persona's typical subtasks**

1. Go to the homepage.

2. Find the link to the sign-up page.
   Goal: get trustworthy and independent advice.

3. Click it.

4. Fill in all his details without any errors.
   Goal: trust them with my information.

5. See the confirmation screen.

6. Receive a confirmation email.

7. Write down user name and password somewhere.

By breaking down this task into sub-tasks, we've already called attention to good error-handling (what happens when Mason enters the wrong information?) and a good confirmation email, two things that are often ignored in web development but are crucial to the successful completion of a task like this.

Now that the task has been analyzed, it becomes easier to make design decisions. Adding design notes to the task at this stage will make the design easier later on:

Note how we haven't said anything specific about the interface yet. If you are already imagining how this website could look, that's good. But avoid writing any details about the interface in your task analysis. Focus on the flow of the task. This part is about getting the task right from a user's point of view. You will design the interface later.

Task analysis is a good way to find out parts of a task that haven't been well supported by the user interface; it often helps you identify new and useful functionality.

**Design and marketing response to persona's task flow**

1. Go to the homepage.
   Marketing note: extra motivation for sign-up could be a special offer.

2. Find the link to the sign-up page.
   Goal: get trustworthy and independent advice.
   Design note: provide visual reassurance.

3. Click it.

4. Fill in all his details without any errors.
   Goal: trust website with personal information.
   Design notes: be careful about asking for sensitive information. Good error-handling is crucial to increase trust.

5. See the confirmation screen.
   Design notes: link this screen with next action: "get familiar with system." Foreshadow all the useful things the user will be able to do now to make sure they will come back.

6. Receive a confirmation email.
   Design notes: also link confirmation email with "get familiar with system" action. Prompt user to write down user name and password.

7. Write down user name and password somewhere.

*Task analysis often helps you identify new and useful functionality*

**How much task analysis do you do for a typical website?**

It depends on the amount of functionality. You don't have to do task analysis for every little thing that people can do on the website—focus on complex or crucial tasks when you are uncertain of the best way to approach them.

*Supporting non-obvious tasks is what sets great websites apart from mediocre ones*

# Turning task analysis into web pages

Using the task analysis, you can now identify the pages of the website and how they will work together.

First, determine which main pages will be needed, and the core tasks they will support, without worrying about interface details. Once these core pages have been developed, turning them into a user interface design will be easy. The advantage of purely focusing on core tasks is that you can already begin testing these pages. Testing early on is crucial. Once the core pages work well, you can start supporting secondary tasks.

So, look at your task analysis, and pick out the core tasks; for example Write Email, Send Email, Add Address to Address Book, and so on, for a web-based email system. Then think about what the core functionality pages on your website will be: these are often the same as the core tasks. A core functionality page on a web-based email system would be "write an email." Write down a name for each core functionality page and the task it supports. Core pages that you can't find a good name for can often be removed or broken down into separate pages. Now test your core page design by running tasks or scenarios through them, to see if they all make sense. Take your task analysis and the scenarios you developed and imagine how a variety of people would use the website with the core pages you have developed.

When the core pages work well with the tasks, add in the additional tasks each page will support, and the additional functionality.

Once all the website pages are laid out in this way, each listing additional tasks, it becomes much easier to design the interface for each screen. The core task defines the interface, and the additional tasks define additional interface elements.

When designing these pages, look out for pages that serve no purpose except to confirm an action, like a thank-you page. These pages often provide possibilities for supporting additional tasks. After sending an email for example, a user may want to complete the additional task of adding an email address to their address book.

*Pages that you can't find a good name for can often be removed or broken down into separate pages*

WRITE EMAIL
-ATTACHMENT
-SIGNATURE

VIEW EMAILS
-DELETE
-MOVE TO FOLDER

READ EMAIL
-REPLY    -ADD TO ADDRESS
-READ NEXT

**INITIAL CORE PAGE DESIGN**
**Sticky notes are very useful for working out the core pages of a website and the functionality on each of them.**

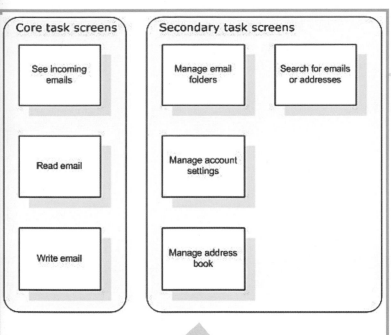

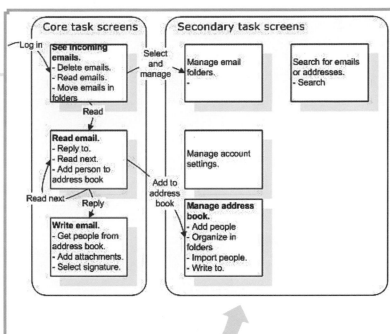

**A CORE PAGE AND A WIREFRAME**
Turning core pages into interface designs is easy, and ensures that the interface is directly related to and focuses on the tasks we wish to support. Further refinements of this interface be necessary, and additional tasks may need supporting. Note that the interface design is just a wireframe at this stage: it shows only the functional elements in an initial layout.

**CORE AND SECONDARY SCREENS**
Each core page represents a task the user will fulfill regularly. To each screen we can add the additional tasks this screen must support. Then it is straightforward to check if our tasks can all be fulfilled easily with this combination of core screens, without needing completed interface designs. Annotations to the visualized layouts (far left) show how a user might move through the screens to complete a task.

*When documenting functionality, use
lots of illustrations and clear language*

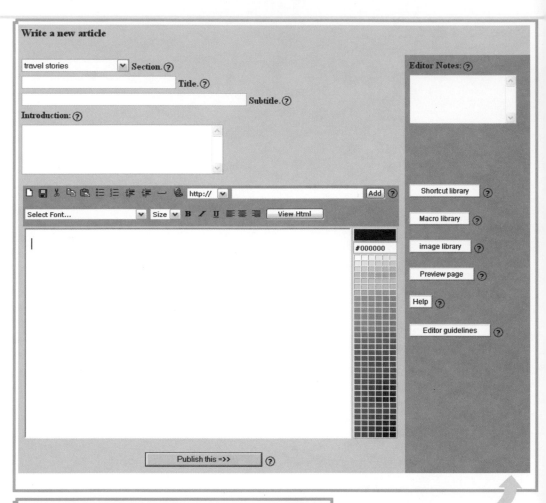

**Write a new article**

travel stories ▾  Section. ⑦

Title. ⑦

Subtitle. ⑦

Introduction: ⑦

Editor Notes: ⑦

http:// ▾                    Add ⑦

Select Font... ▾  Size ▾  **B** *I* U ≡ ≡ ≡    View Html

#000000

Shortcut library ⑦

Macro library ⑦

image library ⑦

Preview page ⑦

Help ⑦

Editor guidelines ⑦

Publish this =>>  ⑦

Yahoo mail and Hotmail both use the
confirmation page after sending an email to
tie in with the task of adding an address to
your address book. However, Hotmail has
the better implementation since the Yahoo
one doesn't indicate whether you already
have this address in your address book, and
then requires an additional click to integrate
it. Yahoo has since adapted this function to
be more user-friendly.

**Your message has been sent to:**     **Save Address:**

peter@poorbuthappy.com                 ☐

                                        Save

Return to Inbox

**Your mail (test) has been sent to:**
petter@poorbuthappy.com
Back to Inbox

**Your message recipient(s):**
Add them to your Address Book **(if they're not already there)**
Invite recipients to use Yahoo! Messenger

ADMINISTRATION SCREEN:
"CREATE A NEW ARTICLE"
The "Create a new article" screen of a
content management system, where
administrators can add new content to a
website. Each core screen should have a
clear title, and be based on a core task.

*Turning core pages into interface designs is easy, and ensures that the interface is directly related to the tasks we wish to support*

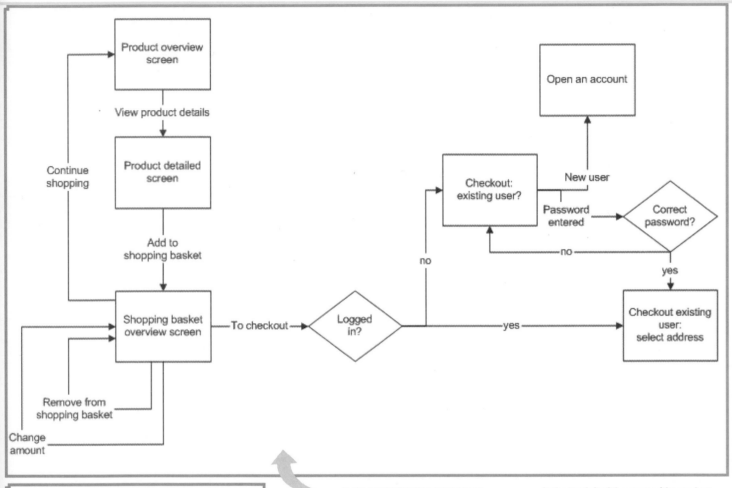

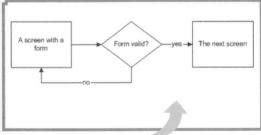

**SIMPLE FLOW CHART**
The boxes in this flowchart represent two pages on the website and the diamond represents a decision: if the form was filled in correctly, go to the next page, or else go back to the first page.

**FLOW CHART ILLUSTRATING PART OF A CHECKOUT PROCESS**
This flow chart illustrates part of a checkout process: from selecting the product, to adding it to the shopping basket, to starting the payment process. Flow charts are a clear way of documenting what should happen at each step of the process. The squares are pages; the diamonds are decisions made by the website. Arrows show what the user has clicked.

At the top-left of the screen, (the product overview screen, containing a list of products), a user goes to the detailed product screen. There they can add this product to the shopping basket, and thus are taken to the shopping basket screen. When they go to the checkout, the website checks if they are already logged in (the first diamond). If so, it proceeds to the checkout page for an existing user where they can select an address. If the user isn't logged in, it proceeds to a page where they can sign in or create a new account.

# Documenting functionality

Functionality decisions have to be communicated to the programmers, designers, and the client. Communicating design decisions is a crucial part of an information architect's job.

A functional specification (or functional spec) is the typical name for the document that explains how a website should work. Sometimes a separate one is written for the client (using less technical language) and for the programmers (containing more technical detail). When documenting functionality, use lots of illustrations (flow charts and wireframes) and clear language. In this section, we'll discuss drawing flow charts and how to write clear functionality descriptions.

### Drawing flow charts

Flow charts are an easy way to express the progression of functionality. They are useful for working out a flow in detail and communicating with technical people who tend to understand flow charts easily.

A flow chart shows steps in a task and alternative routes; for example, what would happen if a user clicks button B instead of button A? What happens if a user clicks this button but isn't logged in? They show pages (as boxes) and decisions in between pages (as diamonds). There is more to flow charts than just boxes and diamonds, but those are the basics. Add in notes if you want to clarify something.

Small (or sometimes large) flow charts are often worked into the functional specification to clarify how something is supposed to work. They are most useful in explaining the flow of subscription processes, shopping baskets, or any functionality that involves a number of screens.

If you are just learning how to do flow charts, talk to your programmers. They are usually familiar with them and will be able to tell you (sometimes in excruciating detail) how to make them. At the very least they hould be able to point you to a good book on the subject.

### Writing functionality descriptions

A functionality description should contain enough detail for the programmer to implement and test it without having to ask too many extra questions. If the client will see it, it should also be clear enough for them to understand.

Functionality descriptions are notorious for being inaccessible and boring because people assume that in order to be precise, they need to use complicated language. Not true. Compare the following two functionality descriptions:

"The system shall provide a clickable link on the article pages that will let the user proceed to a separate version of the page that opens up in a new browser window containing the article presented in a way that is easy to print. The link will be an icon to be designed by the design department."

versus;

"Every article page has a "print this page" icon. When clicked, a new browser window opens up and shows the article in an easy-to-print version (see wireframe 5.2)."

When writing functionality descriptions, ask your programmers how they prefer them. They will use these intensively so if you can provide them with something clear they will have to bother you a lot less with questions.

Functionality descriptions are combined with flow charts and wireframes to make a clear, unambiguous, and easy-to-understand functional specification. See the next chapter on interface design for more about wireframes.

## Conclusion

We have seen how to analyze the tasks people do on a website, and how to turn them into page designs. Designing your functionality around core tasks ensures your main audience goals and tasks, as identified by the research, are reflected in your design. In the next chapter, we will describe how all of this ties in with interface design.

*When writing functionality descriptions, ask your programmers how they prefer them*

## Learning more...

*User and Task Analysis for Interface Design* by Joann T. Hackos and Janice C. Redish is a good book from which to learn more about task analysis.

*Functionality descriptions are notorious for being inaccessible and boring*

**Walk the client through the functional spec**

When you show the functional specification to the client, don't just hand them the document. Organize a meeting and walk them through it. They are bound to have lots of questions and answering them all at once will save you lots of time.

**What is the difference between a flow chart and a sitemap?**

A flow chart illustrates a task—a few pages on the website, and how a user can move through them. It shows the different directions a website can send the user in depending on what they do. A sitemap just shows pages and relationships, no flow or tasks. A flow chart is often put in the functional spec together with a description of the functionality. A document with lots of arrows and diamond boxes is probably a flow chart. Lots of boxes (no diamonds) organized as a tree probably indicates a sitemap.

# Case study: XM Radio
# XMRadio.com

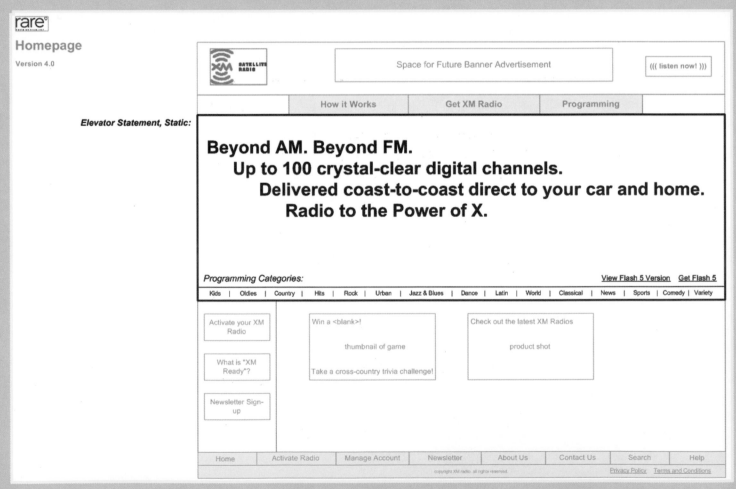

**HOMEPAGE WIREFRAME AND DESIGN**
**The bold element in the wireframe indicates the Flash movie part of the page. This wireframe is an early version of the final page design.**

The information architecture for XMRadio.com was led by Christopher Fahey, the principal information architect at Behavior (www.behaviordesign.com). A lot of market research had been done for this website: the audience they were aiming for was presented in great demographic detail. Christopher proposed additional research that would result in personas, which he finds to be an extremely useful design tool for information architecture (see Chapter 2 for more on personas).

## Conducting additional research

Christopher worked with an in-house user research team. They decided to go out and find people from the target audience in two locations: gadget freaks in electronic stores, and new music lovers in record stores. "Selecting these two locations saved us a lot of hassle trying to find the right people, since we knew our audience could be found in these stores," says Christopher. The teams went out and interviewed about 10 people. They had prepared an interview plan, with questions about topics they wanted to cover. They spent about 30 minutes with each person. Chapter 2 details interviewing techniques.

## Working the interviews into personas

The team then took these interviews, and worked them into six personas. When these were presented to the client, they were happy with the research, and their initial reservations about possibly repeating research that had already been done were resolved. The client was happy to see how the research built on the market research already conducted, yet added a lot of detail that would directly help in making design and information architecture decisions when building the site. Christopher explains: "One of the reasons we included the core market research data next to each persona was to show the client that we were building on the existing research—we weren't starting from scratch doing overlapping or redundant work. They were very pleased with that."

### Behavior
www.behaviordesign.com    XM Radio
User Personas

### Juan, 25: NEW STATION SEEKER    *XM Objective: Increase Awareness*

"I like music variety, the mix. As a music lover, it's all about the variety."

A 25-year-old music enthusiast whose interests span rock, salsa, R&B, house, soft rock and alternative music, **Juan is always looking for the next best fad.** To keep up with new music, he goes to concerts and dance halls weekly. He and his friends also compete to be the first to find up-and-coming DJs or a new house mix. Above all, he must find out about music before it hits the stores. **Juan regularly downloads and trades MP3 hits, and burns CDs for his friends and himself.** In fact, Juan is never without music --- he has six CD players: one in his car, one in his office, two at home (in his bedroom and his living room), a portable one for walking, and one just in case another breaks down.

Juan listens to the radio actively in his car and at work, shifting from station to station. At work as an economic analyst, **Juan now swears by Internet radio** because he has access to countless stations around the world. The music sites he visits most frequently are Columbia House and Sony. He does not go to fan sites because he feels they are geared towards teens. **Juan visits the websites for his favorite local radio stations** (Hot 97, La Mega, and CD101.9) to find out about promotional giveaways (t-shirts and CDs), background information on an artist, and sponsored events, though he is not interested in chat groups. **He's wary about buying things on the web:** he prefers going into specialty record shops, rather than purchasing CDs online.

**NEW STATION SEEKER**
Segment Profile:

| | |
|---|---|
| Male | 49% |
| White | 58 |
| Median Age | 24 |
| Xer | 79 |
| Boomer | 17 |
| Mature | 4 |
| Retired | 3 |
| Median Income | $32.8K |

- Second highest radio listening, including almost three hours on weekend days
- Highest Interest in finding new radio stations
- Strongest Desire to be trendy and on the cutting edge
- Group most likely to buy new technology as soon as it comes out instead of waiting for prices to drop
- Above average involvement with other non-print media
- Media mavens looking for new experiences. Will probably be unimpressed by just the same old stuff with less static. Could be lost if they are not hearing something new and different.

**Juan's Characteristics:**

| | |
|---|---|
| Internet Savvy: | ●●●●○ |
| Listens to terrestrial radio: | ●●●●○ |
| Listens to Internet radio: | ●●●●● |
| Downloads music: | ●●●●● |
| E-commerce comfort: | ●○○○○ |
| Gadget comfort: | ●●●○○ |

**Juan's Preconditions:**

1. Juan owns a Saab 9-3 Viggen and is seeking to replace his existing car radio. On a recent visit to a radio showroom at an electronics store, he became aware of the "XM Ready" label on the Pioneer radio. He first discovered the web site address from a brochure given to him by the salesperson at the store. He's curious about the new technology and the 100 stations, so he visits the site.

**Juan's Goals:**

- What does "XM Ready" mean?
- Does an "XM Ready" radio cost more than a normal radio, even if I never choose to activate the XM Radio features?
- Does XM programming interest me?
- Do the channels accurately reflect the kind of music I like?
- How is XM Radio's programming better than what I can get already from my favorite local stations?
- Why should I pay 10 bucks a month for radio?
- Are there any discount packages?
- Are there commercials?
- What are the DJs like? Can I interact with them?
- Are there any promotions or giveaways?
- Is XM Radio the latest thing on the web?
- Can I hear a sample run?
- Which radio will fit my car?

Page 1 of 2

**PERSONA DESCRIPTION**
Personas were used to make sure the user research was carried through to the design process. They were developed by doing interviews based on initial market research.

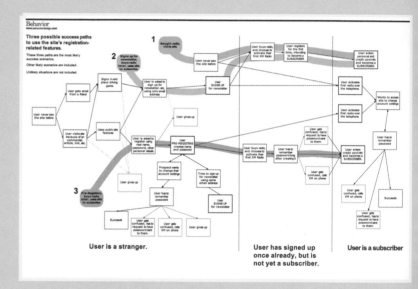

**THE SUCCESS SCENARIOS**
This is an informal map of all the ways the users might go from being curious websurfers to becoming paying customers, including offline methods like using the telephone. It allowed the team to measure the effectiveness of some early site feature ideas, to improve some and reject others. It indicates every risky interaction point, alerting them to potential design and feature problems.

*"Their initial reservations about possibly repeating research that had already been done were resolved"*

*"Without first building a comprehensive list of user goals, I wouldn't have known where to start"*

**XM Radio Service Information**
Find out about what XM Radio is and how it works.

> What is Digital Satellite Radio?
> About **XM-Ready** *(show logo!)*
> Product Catalog
> Frequently-Asked Questions

**THE CONCEPTUAL WIREFRAME**
The first wireframe was a big box containing a lot of elements that might have to go on the homepage. Christopher comments, "By using these conceptual model diagrams, we were able to discuss which elements to remove and which to keep."

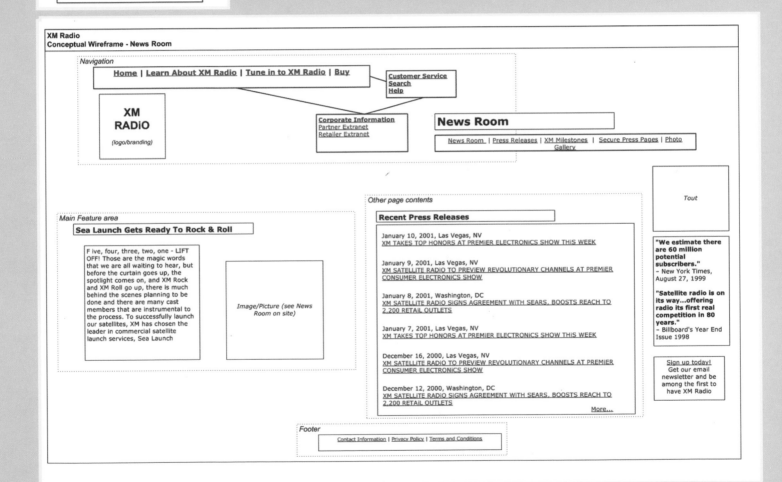

XM Radio
Conceptual Wireframe - News Room

Navigation

Home | Learn About XM Radio | Tune in to XM Radio | Buy

Customer Service
Search
Help

XM
RADiO

*(logo/branding)*

Corporate Information
Partner Extranet
Retailer Extranet

**News Room**

News Room  |  Press Releases  |  XM Milestones  |  Secure Press Pages  |  Photo Gallery

Other page contents

*Tout*

Main Feature area

**Sea Launch Gets Ready To Rock & Roll**

Five, four, three, two, one - LIFT OFF! Those are the magic words that we are all waiting to hear, but before the curtain goes up, the spotlight comes on, and XM Rock and XM Roll go up, there is much behind the scenes planning to be done and there are many cast members that are instrumental to the process. To successfully launch our satellites, XM has chosen the leader in commercial satellite launch services, Sea Launch

*Image/Picture (see News Room on site)*

**Recent Press Releases**

January 10, 2001, Las Vegas, NV
XM TAKES TOP HONORS AT PREMIER ELECTRONICS SHOW THIS WEEK

January 9, 2001, Las Vegas, NV
XM SATELLITE RADIO TO PREVIEW REVOLUTIONARY CHANNELS AT PREMIER CONSUMER ELECTRONICS SHOW

January 8, 2001, Washington, DC
XM SATELLITE RADIO SIGNS AGREEMENT WITH SEARS, BOOSTS REACH TO 2,200 RETAIL OUTLETS

January 7, 2001, Las Vegas, NV
XM TAKES TOP HONORS AT PREMIER ELECTRONICS SHOW THIS WEEK

December 16, 2000, Las Vegas, NV
XM SATELLITE RADIO TO PREVIEW REVOLUTIONARY CHANNELS AT PREMIER CONSUMER ELECTRONICS SHOW

December 12, 2000, Washington, DC
XM SATELLITE RADIO SIGNS AGREEMENT WITH SEARS, BOOSTS REACH TO 2,200 RETAIL OUTLETS

More...

**"We estimate there are 60 million potential subscribers."**
– New York Times, August 27, 1999

**"Satellite radio is on its way...offering radio its first real competition in 80 years."**
– Billboard's Year End Issue 1998

Sign up today!
Get our email newsletter and be among the first to have XM Radio


Contact Information | Privacy Policy | Terms and Conditions

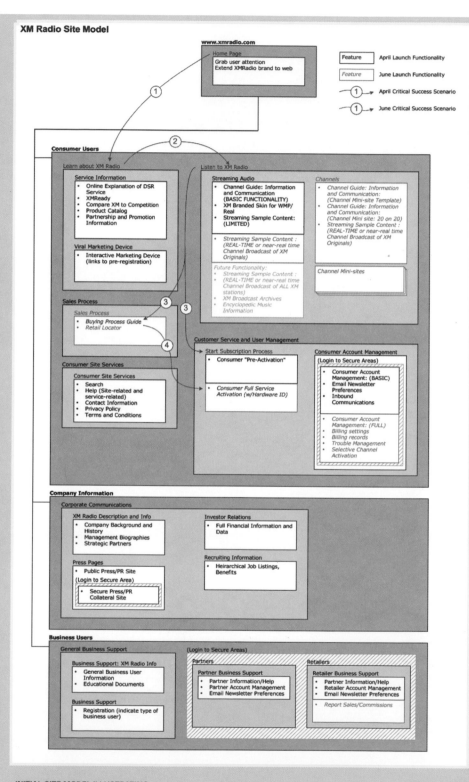

*"We always use usability testing to refine our designs"*

**INITIAL SITE MODEL ILLUSTRATING
SUCCESS SCENARIOS**
This model illustrates sections of the website
and how the users would navigate it
successfully. Success scenarios are used to
discuss the structure of the website.

## Using personas for information architecture

The most useful element when constructing the information architecture were the goals listed with each persona. "You can see how some of those questions lead directly to a certain button on the website," says Christopher. "I came up with the three main navigation concepts almost immediately. It just seemed to fit. Without first building a comprehensive list of user goals, I wouldn't have known where to start. Using the personas, the navigation practically suggested itself."

There was a lot of discussion about the Programming label: "We were afraid that Programming might make people believe this was a website for computer programmers." But usability testing showed that users had no problems with this label.

## User testing to refine designs

"We always use usability testing to refine our designs," says Christopher, "it is a fantastic tool." They showed the designs to a number of people, and asked them to try to use them. "The testing showed us that some of the internal pages of the website did a terrible job at explaining the XM Radio concept to people." The team started implementing daily fixes while conducting the tests, presenting refined prototypes on each successive day of testing. "The usability testing showed us how little we could assume about how much consumers know about the product and service," says Christopher. "I think every page is in some way colored by this insight."

**EARLY HOMEPAGE DESIGN**
This design was adjusted during and after a round of usability testing that preceded the final design. Notice how the labels of the top navigation were simplified and clarified in the final design.

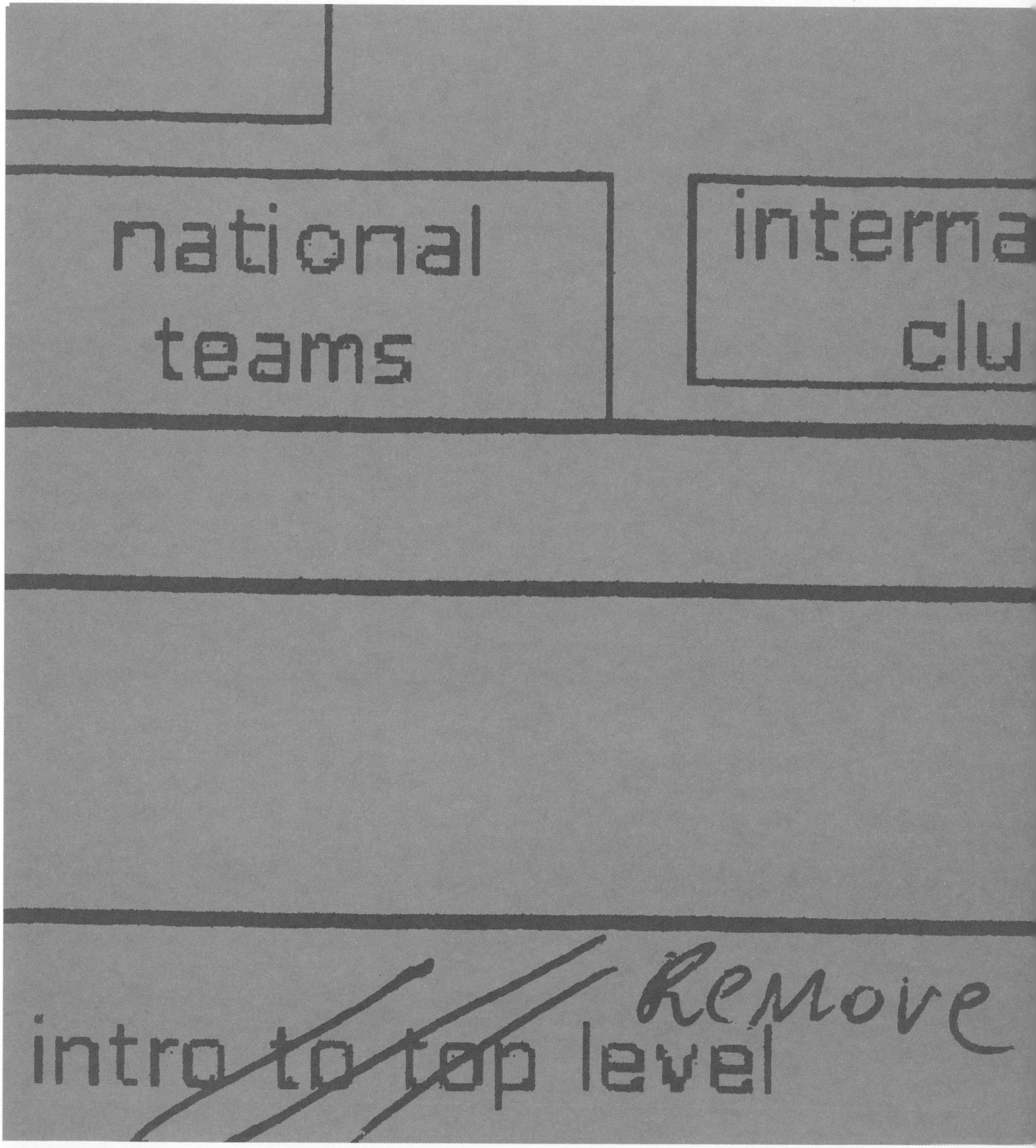

national
teams

interna
clu

intro to top level *Remove*

# Interface design

protection & other gear

**5**

This chapter is about interface design: the part of designing a website that deals with what interface elements go where on a page. We won't talk about colors, branding, or fonts.

What is the difference between interface design and visual design? It's a blurry line; both deal with the stuff on the page, but interface design tries to make a page functional, self-explanatory, and compatible with user goals; while visual design tries to assure a certain look and feel—a style. These definitions are often discussed in great depth on certain mailing lists, but don't really matter in this chapter. So feel free to disagree with my definition and enjoy the chapter anyway.

The interface is the part of a system that we interact with. It is the connection between the company behind a website (its people, its systems, its information) and the user.

An interface should be useful, enjoyable, easy-to-use, and efficient. Useful means that it should support what you want to do on the website—your tasks. Enjoyable and easy-to-use mean just what they say. Efficient means fast and avoiding mistakes. Which is more important depends on the situation. Useful is almost always more important than all the others. Easy-to-use, enjoyable, and efficient can have various importance, depending on the situation. Sometimes it is better to make a task enjoyable than it is to make it efficient: if you are doing the task for fun there is not much point in making it highly efficient but boring. However, if a company wants to save money and have their employees use the intranet faster, efficiency becomes more important than enjoyment.

# Wireframes

Wireframes or page schematics are simplified page layouts. They show the elements on the page but not the visual design.

The purpose of wireframes is to show how a page will work independently of the visual design. The advantage of using them is that they allow for quick iterations: they are easy to make and adjust, and they keep you focused on the elements on the page, so you can get those right before starting the visual design.

The information architect and the visual designer should develop wireframes together if these roles are filled by separate people. The information architect brings his or her knowledge of organization schemes and user and business goals, while the visual designer brings insights about page layout and interface design techniques.

Wireframes are great tools for client communication. When reading a description of a website in a functional spec, it is hard to imagine what the website will look like. A wireframe is easy to understand.

Make sure the client understands that these are not visual designs, especially if your wireframes look good. Stories abound of clients who assumed the wireframe was the visual design and complained later when things were changed. When discussing wireframes with your client, tell them you will discuss visual elements (like color, visual treatment of interface widgets, and so on) later on. The best way of dealing with this confusion is to show the client a visual design next to a wireframe, and explain the difference. If you don't have a visual design yet, use one from a previous project. An additional risk comes when the client distributes the wireframes inside their organization—don't let them. The people who see these assume this is the visual design, and confusion is guaranteed.

Wireframes are often made in illustration programs. It's useful to build a library of page elements so you can drag and drop pages together. The book's website 🖥 provides some Visio stencils for doing wireframes. Refrain from visual design; instead of designing a logo just put a box saying "logo". Instead of designing a navigation item, just use a box with the name of that item. Wireframes are usually done in black and white, to avoid attracting attention to color schemes.

*Useful, enjoyable, easy-to-use ,and efficient. Which is more important depends on the situation*

*Make sure the client understands wireframes are not visual designs*

**Don't design your wireframes**

Wireframes are used for discussions, testing, and communicating requirements, not to illustrate design. If you add design elements like colors or fonts to your wireframes you run the risk that they will be mistaken for the finished designs, and you will have a lot of explaining to do.

**Wireframes in HTML**

You can make your wireframes in any program you feel comfortable with—it doesn't really matter. If you do them in HTML however, you increase the risk that they will be mistaken for real designs because you will be adding the HTML "look" to them. Add a clear disclaimer explaining that wireframes aren't visual designs.

"Wireframes are becoming an integral part of the design process. What our designers have realized is that wireframes are not designs, and are not carved in stone. We use them to create discussion, understand content placement, and help formulate the direction that the design should take. On several recent projects, we've worked with designers to create the wireframes, enabling us to notice potential pitfalls before time was spent designing. It's much easier to change a wireframe than a finished design."
**Jared Folkmann, Information Architect**

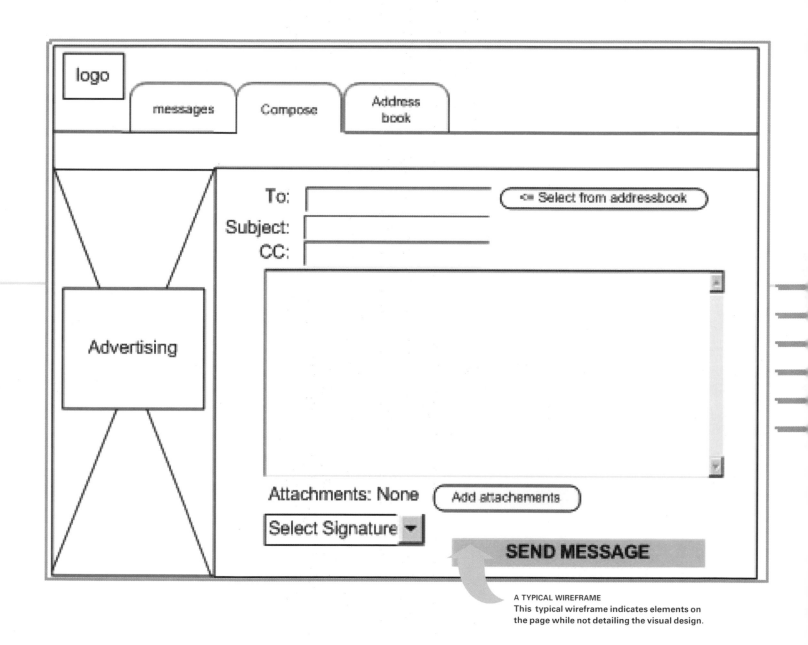

**A TYPICAL WIREFRAME**
This typical wireframe indicates elements on
the page while not detailing the visual design.

*"We've worked with designers to create wireframes,
enabling us to notice potential pitfalls before time was
spent designing"*

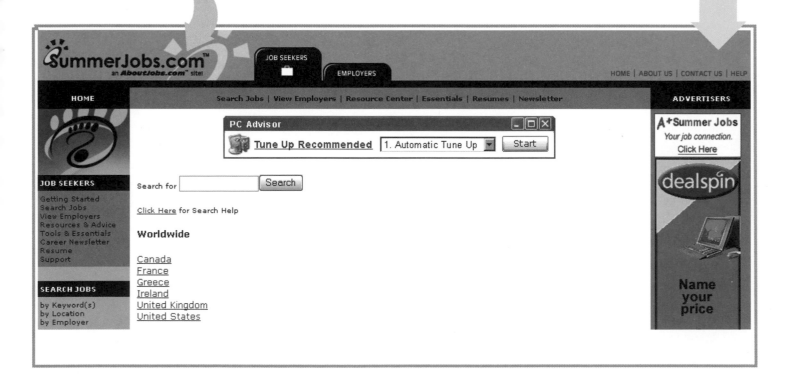

**www.** SUMMERJOBS.COM
Wireframes are only an indication of which elements should go on the page. Visual design determines how they go on the page (the wireframe above isn't the original, it was made as an example by looking at the live website).

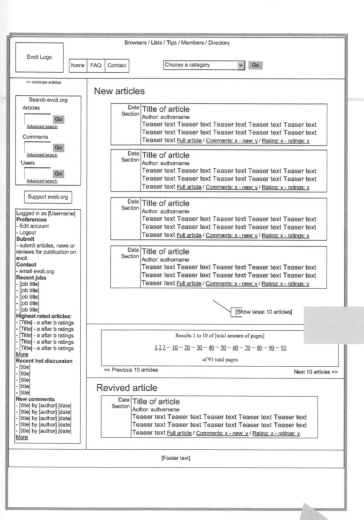

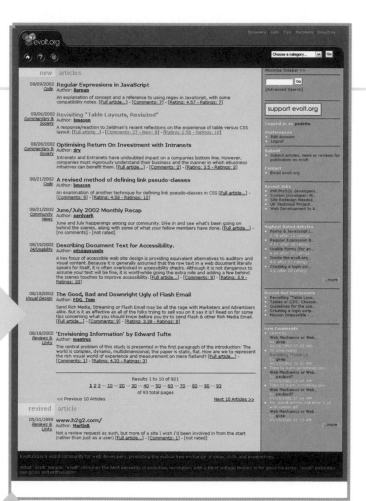

www. EVOLT.COM

**This wireframe (reconstructed by analyzing the evolt.org homepage shown above right) illustrates how wireframes relate to the visual design. They indicate elements on the page and labels, but don't fix the visual elements of the design. Notice how in the wireframe the navigation bar is on the left, while in the finished design it is on the right. Wireframes are usually constructed for all the main pages of a website.**

*Instead of designing a logo just put a box saying "logo"*

## Interface objects

An interesting way of thinking of an interface is that it consists of objects that can be presented in different ways. An object is just a thing that appears on your website: it could be an article, a navigation menu, or a shopping basket.

All websites consist of a number of objects like this, and different screens will present different views of these objects. One view of an article object could be the complete article; another view could be a short teaser for the article on the homepage. One view of the shopping basket could be the icon at the top of every page; another view could be the last page in the shopping basket before paying.

Designing a website then becomes like playing with building blocks: you first design each object (an article, a shopping basket) separately, and then combine them on pages.

The power of this way of thinking is that you can now design the different views of these objects separately from the pages, and focus on developing a consistent visual identity for each object over different views. An article will always have the same "look," whether it is an article teaser on the homepage or an article title in the search results. It also gives you a nice balance between flexibility and consistency: you can combine elements on a page in any way you like, but you will always keep the same look for these elements.

To use this way of designing, simply make a list of objects, and for each object make a list of different views. Then design all the views for this object, keeping a consistent visual treatment for each object. Finally, combine the objects into pages.

### Article teaser

**Title of the article**  Date

Lorem ipsum dolor sit amet, consetetur sadipscing elitr, sed diam nonumy eirmod tempor invidunt ut labore et

Read more

### Article short teaser

**Title of the article**  Date

### Complete article

**Title of the article**  
Date, author

Print this page

Lorem ipsum dolor sit amet, consetetur sadipscing elitr, sed diam nonumy eirmod tempor invidunt ut labore et

Picture

Lorem ipsum dolor sit amet, consetetur sadipscing elitr, sed diam nonumy eirmod tempor invidunt ut labore et dolore magna aliquyam erat, sed diam voluptua. At vero eos et accusam et justo duo dolores et ea rebum. Stet clita kasd gubergren, no sea takimata sanctus est Lorem ipsum dolor sit amet. Lorem ipsum dolor sit amet, consetetur sadipscing elitr, sed diam nonumy eirmod tempor invidunt ut labore et dolore magna aliquyam erat, sed diam voluptua. At vero eos et accusam et justo duo dolores et ea rebum. Stet clita kasd gubergren, no sea takimata sanctus est Lorem ipsum dolor sit amet. Lorem ipsum dolor sit amet, consetetur sadipscing elitr, sed diam nonumy eirmod tempor invidunt ut labore et dolore magna aliquyam erat, sed diam voluptua. At vero eos et accusam et justo duo dolores et ea rebum. Stet clita kasd gubergren, no sea takimata sanctus est Lorem ipsum dolor sit amet.

# Sending post from Colombia

*In these days of email, sometimes sending post is still the way to go*

More articles like this in the [daily life](#) section.

September 2002 - by Judith in Medellin

Sending mail from Colombia should be a simple, straightforward experience. After all, your letters/postcards to send home are neatly addressed, you've got the money to buy stamps, what could possibly go wrong?

The answer is, quite a lot. Firstly, after you've been here a while, you start noticing a distinct lack of post boxes. That's because they don't exist here. Once you've got over that minor shock, you locate your nearest post office. There are two types. The state-run, Adpostal, and the private ones, Deprisa. Letters sent with Adpostal cost from 3,200 pesos each and can take anything from one week to one month to get to their destination (especially if it's in Europe). If it's any further away expect an even longer arrival time – **a letter I sent to Australia once arrived exactly two months later**. Letters sent from private post offices cost about double the amount at state-run places but there's no guarantee they will get there any quicker – although they are supposedly more secure. The choice is yours.

[Visa overstay.](#)
[Visas - overview](#)
[Getting married](#)

### Culture and daily life
[Betty La Fea](#)
[differences](#)
[a marriachi serenade](#)
[Colombian tv](#)
[Tips on life in colombia](#)
[Changing money in Colombia](#)
[Locating someone in Colombia](#)
[Queueing up in South America](#)
[South American toilets](#)
[Colombia High](#)
[Sending post from Colombia](#)

### Working and teaching English
[private students](#)
[Schools in Medellin.](#)
[work safety](#)

## Sending post from Colombia
*In these days of email, sometimes sending post is still the way to go*
Some dos and donts on sending post to Colombia [more](#)

**DIFFERENT ENTRY POINTS TO AN ARTICLE**
**An object like an article will often appear several times on the same website, in different circumstances. Work out how these objects will appear first, and then combine them into page designs.**

**THREE DIFFERENT VIEWS OF AN ARTICLE**
**When designing your interface using interface objects, you construct different views of each object. An article can be viewed in the search results (in which case only a short teaser is shown), or on an overview page of articles (in which case a long teaser is shown), or on the article page itself. Working with interface objects makes it easier to achieve a consistent look for each object. An object is any element that appears on the website: a shopping basket, an article, a picture, or a sign-up page.**

**Using interface objects**

When trying out this technique, don't design the interface objects in isolation without considering the web pages. A web page has a visual balance between its elements, so jump back and forth between page and object design.

## Iteration works

Iteration is crucial to design; every designer knows that the first version of a design isn't usually the best one. Refining designs based on various types of feedback makes for great designs instead of average ones.

However, making changes to a detailed visual design is expensive because it takes a lot of time—that's why we use wireframes. They let you play around with the elements on a page, the labels for them, and different interface solutions without spending a lot of time on visual design.

Prototyping means building a version of a website and trying it out, and is probably the single most efficient thing you can do when designing an interface. Build a rough interface, see if people understand it, and make adjustments. You will see prototyping doesn't have to be time-intensive or expensive. The crucial factor when choosing a prototyping technique is: can you make changes easily?

So, when you begin designing a website, don't begin with a beautiful design for the homepage. First make sketches and prototypes and iterate through them until you are confident you have something that works.

## Paper prototyping

Because of the importance of quick changes in prototyping, paper has become the most popular prototyping tool for interface design. Many of the best interface design companies use this technique. Don't underestimate paper prototyping because it seems simple; that simplicity is exactly where its power lies.

To do paper prototyping, sketch the pages of the interface onto pieces of paper, then grab some people (anyone will do, although it is always better to get people from your target audience) and ask them to fulfill a task supported by the interface. For an email interface that could be Send Email. For a shopping site it could be Find Item. Give them a pencil, and ask them to imagine the pieces of paper as computer screens and to use the pen to "click" on things. People are surprisingly flexible and imaginative, and most people get it straight away.

When they click, you play the computer and take the paper away and replace it with a new paper, simulating a browser. If it takes you some time to find the right page to give them, just say "we're on a slow connection here." Ask them to think out loud, and to comment on what they are doing. If they don't start talking out loud straight away, remind them. Only interrupt them to ask questions; never tell them how to do something. Remember, you are here to find out where things go wrong, so if they fail that's a good thing. Ask them things like: "Why did you click there?" or "What were you expecting on this page?" Remember the audience research techniques of Chapter 2.

*Prototyping is probably the single most efficient thing you can do when designing an interface*

*Paper has become the most popular prototyping tool for interface design*

**Even sketches can be tested**

Even rough sketches on paper can be tested: ask people to use them as if they were real websites. You will be surprised at how much you'll learn—and plans on paper are easy to adapt, so this is a perfect time to do lots of quick iterations.

PAPER PROTOTYPING: THE DESIGNER MADE SOME QUICK SKETCHES OF THE INTERFACE  TO TEST THEM OUT…

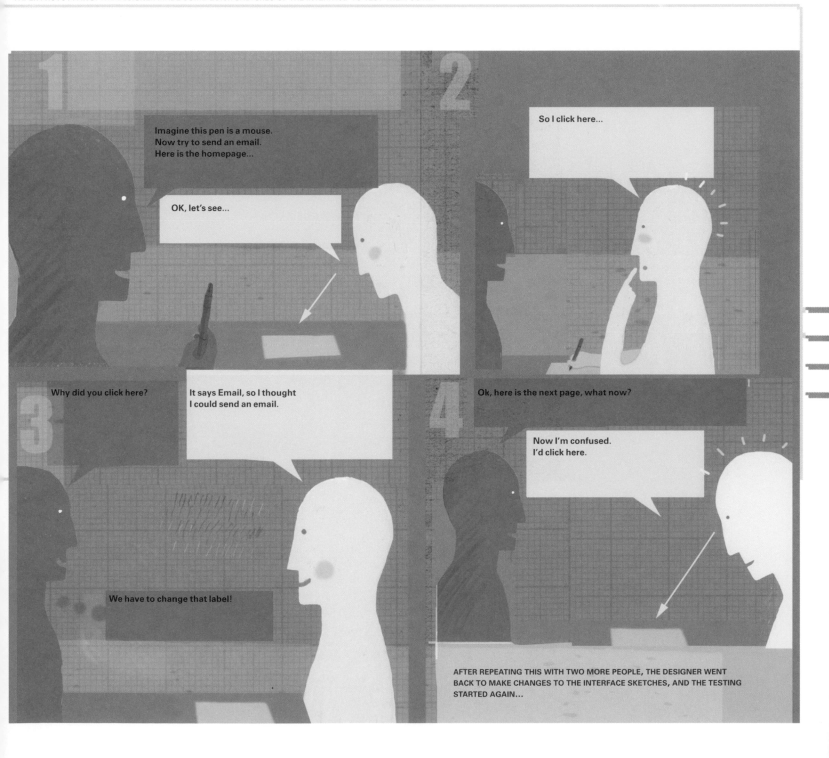

When you have tested a prototype with some people, draw your conclusions and make changes, then test again. Flexibility is key, so don't be afraid to change things in the middle of a prototyping session. Feel free to change the name of links, or to add drop-downs, or make any changes if you feel they will improve things. Since we're working on paper, changes are easy. The whole idea of the process is to make changes until things work.

Paper prototypes can be drawn as sketches, or worked out in a drawing program. Just remember that flexibility is the most important thing. Use sticky notes to add interactive elements like drop-downs or pop-up menus. When you want to change something on the prototype, just write it on there. You will think of many small changes to make during the tests, so feel free to make them during testing.

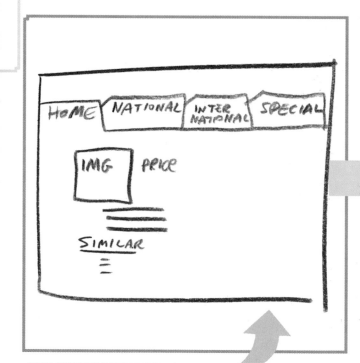

**INITIAL INTERFACE SKETCH OF THE PRODUCT DETAIL PAGE**
Initial sketches of the interface can be quickly worked into paper prototypes.

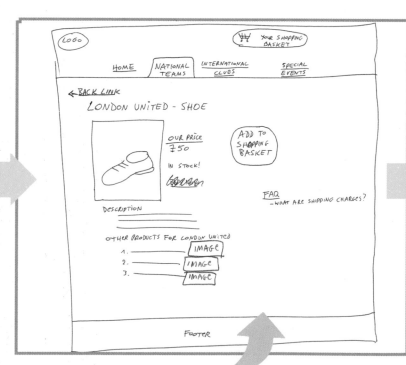

**INITIAL PAPER PROTOTYPE**
Paper prototyping is the one of the fastest prototyping techniques available. Sketch the interface on a piece of paper, and test it straight away. Try to use the right labels. Ask someone to play as if this was a real website, and ask them to use it: where would they click? What information would they expect on this page? Make notes, and after the exercise go back and make some more changes. Some people use a whiteboard to do these initial prototypes since it is even faster to erase and change things.

## HTML prototypes

HTML prototypes are working examples of a website. They can be useful tools to explore new concepts, but are generally costly to develop. When explaining an idea for an interface widget to a client, HTML prototypes can be very convincing. Use paper for the initial prototyping work, but only move to working HTML prototypes when you have already done extensive paper prototyping and wireframes. Working prototypes can be especially useful for showing, testing, and explaining unusual interface widgets.

## Conclusion

Interface design is another first step towards a finished design, and is more about the elements on a page and their relationships than about the aesthetics of colors and visual design. Iteration and prototyping is crucial to good interface design, and the cheapest and fastest techniques are often the best.

*When explaining an idea for an unusual interface widget to a client, HTML prototypes can be very convincing*

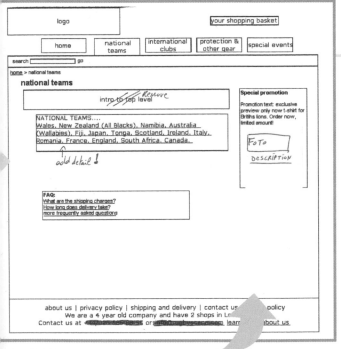

**FURTHER PAPER PROTOTYPING**
**Once a wireframe has been designed, further paper prototyping can be done. Print out the wireframes and test it again by asking people to use the paper as a website. Don't be afraid to make notes and changes—that's the whole point of this exercise. You can use pens or sticky notes to change things in the interface during testing.**

"We were designing a website containing speech therapy resources. During a walkthrough of a prototype with users, we were discussing the link labels. One of the users said, 'Of course the actual labels will include an indication of which regional dialect the resource is in, won't they?' This very important piece of information was so obvious to the users that they had never mentioned it and as developers we didn't have specialist knowledge of the domain, so had never asked the question. Prototypes are useful because they allow the user to see what your design means in practice, revealing any misunderstandings or false assumptions as well as confirming good elements of the design."
**Daniel Cunliffe, Senior Lecturer in Multimedia Computing**

# Case study: Lycos Asia
**lycosasia.com**

| Use Case ID: | M007 | | |
|---|---|---|---|
| Use Case Name: | Forward Mail | | |
| Created By: | | Last Updated By: | N/A |
| Date Created: | | Date Last Updated: | N/A |
| Actor: | Lycos Asia Contact user | | |
| Description: | To forward the mail from the mailbox to other recipients | | |
| Preconditions: | Mails to be forward are in the mailbox | | |
| Post conditions: | Mails forwarded successfully to other recipients | | |
| Normal Flow of Events: | 1.  Open mail to be forwarded<br>2.  Specify recipients for the mail<br>3.  Send the mail | | |
| Alternative Flow: | AF1. No recipients specified | | |
| Special Requirements: | 1.  Multiple mail including attachment can be forwarded from mailbox with a single action button. | | |
| Assumptions: | N/A | | |
| Notes and Issues: | N/A | | |

**THE DEVELOPMENT OF LYCOS ASIA**
**Information architecture techniques helped to turn the high-level requirements ("Ability to send multiple emails," for example) into page designs. First, task analysis was used to better understand the tasks, then work was done on the interface flow and elements and wireframes were developed. After the wireframes came HTML prototypes, which were finally refined into finished designs.**

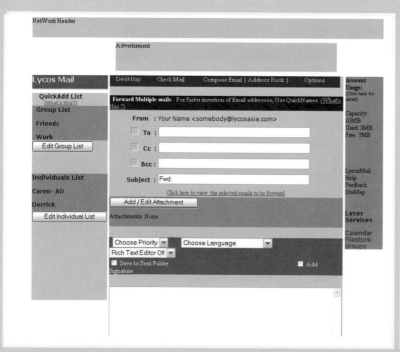

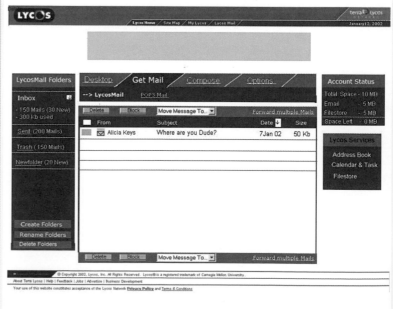

When Lycos Asia were redesigning their website, Melvin Kumar was responsible for the design of the user interface. He used wireframes and paper prototypes to design an efficient user interaction. Melvin comments "I had to make a lot of design decisions in a relative short time span. Using information architecture techniques helped me greatly."

Lycos Asia is a typical portal site, aimed at paying customers in South Asia, which provides the usual functionality like email, address books, and calendars. The challenge in this project was to take the fairly high-level requirements and audience analysis that Melvin was given, and turn them into an effective interface design.

He used task analysis to refine the high-level requirements he was given. "I looked at the requirements, which were as high level as ability to forward multiple emails, and then analyzed the steps a user would have to take to actually do that." Then he defined the interaction flow and the interface elements. "Once the interface elements and the interaction flow were defined, I started designing them into the paper prototypes." Paper prototypes are a common way of cheaply testing and adjusting user interfaces. These paper prototypes led to wireframes, which in turn led to the final designs. Chapter 4 gives an explanation of task analysis and Chapter 5 provides tips on wireframes and paper prototyping.

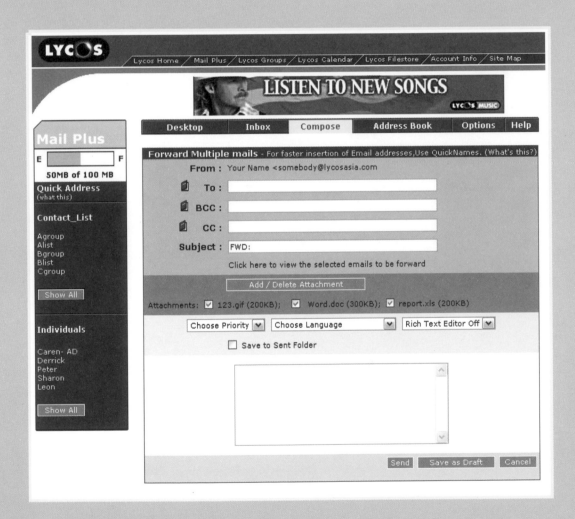

*Using information architecture techniques helps to make lots of design decisions in a short time span*

# Final word

Let's face it: after almost 10 years of web development, many websites are still pretty bad. A typical website of any complexity will reveal hundreds of usability problems after only a few days of testing. Content is written as advertising copy. We redesign our sites every year or so. Information architecture decisions are made without even realizing a decision has been made. Slapping a logo and the corporate colors on a site is often considered a sufficient branding effort. The list of problems goes on. Users end up lost and frustrated.

There is a problem with the way websites are built. Successful websites combine the best of visual design, business strategy, programming, content writing, marketing and branding, usability, and information architecture.

All these disciplines must work together effectively, yet they often have drastically different ways of understanding the world and end up restricting each other. But different perspectives can be a good thing: they can work together to give us a richer, more textured, understanding of what is going on. With this book, I have tried to provide some insight into the way an information architect looks at the web, and to narrow the gap between information architects and visual designers. There are more gaps to be narrowed though, and more bridges to be built.

Good designers know that understanding their audience and designing for them is no threat to their creativity. Information architects are learning about the rich inheritance of the design and marketing professions. Few business people truly appreciate that technology isn't a commodity. The best programmers understand that technology is not an end, it is a means. Usability specialists are leaving their ivory towers and understand that ease of use is not the only factor that matters in an interface. Marketers are starting to understand that designing a successful product requires different skills than selling one.

The teams that really learn these lessons are the ones that will develop websites that will delight us with their elegance, ease of use, beauty, and usefulness. The web is young. We have much to learn from each other.

*After almost 10 years of web development, many websites are still pretty bad*

# Bibliography

If you want to learn more about information architecture you're in luck. A number of excellent books have been published. If you are low on cash, check out the websites of these books. Many contain sample chapters that can help you decide which one to buy. If you can spare the money, buy them all. Each one contains excellent information and a different perspective.

**If you are new to the world of information architecture, buy these three books to get you started:**
*Information Architecture for the World Wide Web*
by Louis Rosenfeld and Peter Morville
(O'Reilly & Associates, 2002)
www.oreilly.com/catalog/infotecture2

*Information Architecture:Blueprints for the Web*
by Christina Wodkte
(New Riders Publishing, 2002)
www.eleganthack.com

*Don't Make Me Think: A Common Sense Approach to Usability*
by Steve Krug
(Que, 2000)
www.sensible.com/buythebook.html

**Also of interest:**
*Practical Information Architecture: A Hands-on Approach to Structuring Successful Websites*
by Eric Reiss
(Addison Wesley Publushing, 2002)
Still relevant despite being somewhat older, this book positions information architecture in a business context, and gives lots of practical advice. It misses the latest developments in information architecture but provides a refreshing perspective.

**Books that are not directly related to information architecture but you should still own:**

*The Elements of the User Experience: User-Centred Design for the Web*
by Jesse James Garrett
(New Riders Publishing, 2002)
www.jjg.net/elements
This book defines the user experience and explains which elements contribute to creating a great one.

*The Design of Sites: Patterns, Principles, and Processes for Crafting a Customer-Centered Web Experience*
by Douglas K. van Duyne, James A. Landay, Jason I. Hong
(Addison Wesley Professional, 2002)
A practical book that provides best practices in the form of design patterns. Use it while designing sites (especially things like shopping baskets) to make sure you are not missing any best practices. Excellent!

**If you own all these and are hungry for more:**
The website with this book provides links to many others
http://iabook.com

# *www.* Webography

The information architecture community is a generous one. You can find all sorts of treasures online: the latest insights and discussions can be found on various weblogs and mailing lists, and several leading companies and consultants make their presentations, and even templates for their deliverables, available for free. Time on these websites will be well spent.

### Companies and consultants

Adaptive Path, a leading user experience consulting company, must be of the most generous companies out there. On their website they provide articles, tutorials, and freely downloadable templates for specific deliverables for information architects.
www.adaptivepath.com

Lou Rosenfeld (one of the authors of *Information Architecture for the World Wide Web*) is a leading information architecture consultant, and maintains a weblog. He also provides freely downloadable presentations on the website.
http://louisrosenfeld.com

Amy J. Warner is another leading information architecture consultant and also provides free articles and downloadable presentations on her website.
www.lexonomy.com

### Weblogs

There are hundreds of weblogs of interest to the budding information architect. Weblogs are online diaries, and many of the leading information architects maintain one.

IASlash (http://iaslash.com) is one of the most focused ones. To find links to more weblogs, visit the website at http://iabook.com

### Mailing lists

There are various mailing lists of interest. The two you should subscribe to are the SIGIA-L mailing list and the AIFIA members mailing list (see below).

The SIGIA-L mailing list is archived at
www.info-arch.org/lists/sigia-l

### Professional organizations

The Asilomar Institute for Information Architecture (AIfIA) is a non-profit volunteer organization dedicated to advancing and promoting information architecture. It provides lots of services and information for the information architect.
www.aifia.org

# Acknowledgments

I found out about the information architecture community that gave me so much through Peter Merholz's weblog (http://peterme.com). That led me to Jesse James Garret's site (http://www.jjg.net), which led to Christina Wodtke's site (http://eleganthack.com). Then came the first edition of *Information Architecture for the World Wide Web* by Louis Rosenfeld and Peter Morville. I haven't looked back since.

Many generous people gave me tips, ideas, reviewed chapters, and generally helped me out while I was writing this book. If you read something you don't think is quite right, it is probably because I ignored their good advice.

Thanks to Alice Calabrese, Anders Ramsey, Andrew Heaton, Andrew Hinton, Ariel Guersenzvaig, Berna Tural, Beth Archibald Tang, Bonnie Becker Ramsey, Carl Smith, Chris C. Martin, Chris Poterala, Christina Wodtke, Christopher Fahey, Cinnamon Melchor, Cristina Mateo, Dan Brown, Daniel Cunliffe, David Charles Ptak, Dennis Huston, Derek Rogerson, Donna Maurer, Eric Scheid, Faith D'Lamater, Garrick Van Buren, George Olsen, Gordon Montgomery, Heather Johnson, Heidi Johnson, Jared Folkmann, Jason K. McDonald, Jeff Lash, Jess McMullin, Jodi Bollaert, my editor Kate Shanahan, Katherine Marshak, Katie Ware, Kelli Bernard, Kristiana Burk, Lisa Mullineaux, Liz Danzico, Lyle Kantrovich, Margaret Hanley, Mark Lawrence, Martyn Perks, Mary Lukaniski, Melvin Kumar, Michael Brown, Mike Steckel, Patty Curthoys, Paul Martin, Peter Boersma, Rachel Abrams, Reid Booth, Richard Hill, Richard M. Oppedisano, Sarah Holmes, Shelley Goodwin, Stuart Church, Sunir Shah, Tal Herman, Theresa Ross, Thomas Donehower, Todd Wilkens, Victor Lombardi, Will Schroeder, and Withney Quesenbery.

I owe each of you a few drinks at least. My apologies for those I forgot to mention.

Thanks also to RotoVision, my publishers, especially to my editors Kate Shanahan and Leonie Taylor, and art director Luke Herriott. Many thanks also to Eirik Bøe for designing this book.

Finally, thank you Maria, for putting up with me during the summer of 2002 in New York City when I wrote most of this book. I will love you forever.